Organizing for Learning: Toward the 21st Century

Edited by
Herbert J. Walberg
John J. Lane

Executive Director:	Scott D. Thomson
Director of Publications:	Thomas F. Koerner
Associate Director:	Carol Bruce
Technical Editor:	Eugenia Cooper Potter

ISBN 0-88210-223-0

National Association of Secondary School Principals
1904 Association Drive, Reston, Virginia 22091
(703) 860-0200

Contents

Foreword

Welcome to a world class tour of possibilities for improving the structure of schools as we head toward the 21st century.

In this monograph, 12 authors offer their perspectives on the essential components of good schools. Each vision is unique, yet common elements appear and reappear throughout the pages.

One interesting commonality is the tension expressed between institutional structure and personal values. What holds an organization together—a common outlook or a clever framework for action, or a modicum of both?

Another issue that surfaces in these essays centers on the rising expectations of society for school achievement on one hand and the clear need for making learning more student specific on the other. Perhaps the requirements are compatible.

Organizing for Learning provides a capsule view of the major current proposals for improving schooling. It is a remarkably good piece of work. Furthermore, it offers the practitioner a ready menu of ideas from which to arrange a personal vision of the best school in a specific community.

Particular appreciation for this work goes to co-editors and authors Herbert J. Walberg and John J. Lane. Our thanks also to James W. Keefe, director of research at NASSP, and to the members of the NASSP Curriculum Council who helped plan this publication.

Scott D. Thomson
Executive Director
National Association of Secondary
School Principals

Introduction

HERBERT J. WALBERG AND JOHN J. LANE

NEW AND OLD forms of organizing secondary schools are competing for principals' attention and action. These forms range from the New England boarding school to computer-based managerial approaches. At various times, the organization of schools may be pressured by nationally perceived educational needs, state legislation, and central-office directives; school staff or departmental decisions; and student and community preferences.

Initiatives of individual schools may conflict with central office enterprises, board ambitions, and state mandates. Parent and community involvement may challenge school staff and departmental decision making. Can we see at the center a well-informed, analytic visionary—the principal who brings forth a resolution? Or at least keeps a lid on the pot?

The last wave of school reform tended to impose a degree of curriculum and instructional uniformity on schools, particularly in the South. It seems likely, however, that the future will bring greater "voice and choice" to people within schools and neighborhoods. As a consequence, schools may have opportunities to become more varied and diverse.

Groups of educational leaders, parents, and students may have distinctive preferences; and some may be able to carry out their personal and collective visions. At the same time, of course, they will need to contend with the forces of tradition and pressures toward standardization such as federal regulations of special programs, statewide expenditure formulas, and state and national testing programs.

Within such constraints, what are some chief proposals for school organization? What are their features? Their advantages and disadvantages? How are they intended to encourage learning effectiveness and excellence, equality of opportunity, and diversity? What are the principal's role and the roles of others—including teachers, parents, and students? These are the questions this book is intended to answer.

In thinking about prospective authors who could answer such questions, we tried—with the help of NASSP's Curriculum Council—to discover those with authoritative knowledge of various exemplary forms of organization who could describe the schools they envision and, in some cases, depict actual practices. Fortunately, nearly every invited author accepted our invitation.

In our request for a chapter, we wrote:

> We expect that the authors will be gentle advocates and point out the good points of the forms of organization about which they write; but they should not be zealots. An even-handed objective approach will be appreciated and the mention of a few problems and difficulties the schools face.

We think the authors largely achieved what we asked; and we are delighted with the range of approaches represented.

Exemplary Forms of School Organization

Our purpose in this introduction is to set forth a few highlights of the chapters, to invite the reader's interest, and to expose several themes and issues that run throughout the chapters. It is impossible immediately to absorb all the authors have to offer; we need to ruminate on what they say and reflect on our own experience.

The Essential School

Schools are neither exactly alike nor the same from year to year. But Theodore Sizer finds that good schools balance the claims of national values against the interests of their immediate communities and the special creations of their faculties. Rather than serving as models, such schools adhere to common principles such as: students should master an essential set of skills and areas of knowledge; the school's goals should apply to all students; and teachers should perceive themselves as generalists first.

James Madison School

What are the elements of a sound secondary school curriculum? What kind of curriculum allows for equality of opportunity and access? Former U.S. Secretary of Education William Bennett exemplifies his views on these urgent questions in his vision for the American high school. Mindful that youngsters tend to perform according to expectations, his four-year curriculum aims to include all students yet challenge even the best.

A Site-Managed School

Can schools and central offices strike a balance between autonomy and control? Based on research and a bold legislative initiative for the Chicago Public Schools, John Lane and Herbert Walberg describe efforts to devolve responsibility to principals, teachers, and parents. Such decentralization may present serious problems and great opportunities; but it appears that informed, responsible decision making at the school site may be a key to success.

Mandate-Responsive Schools

Arthur Steller challenges us to reconsider the widespread notion that the school is the best unit for change. Spelling out problems of this approach, he argues that lasting school improvement involves a gradual empowerment of principals and staff that begins at the top. In support of his position, he shows how this approach has been applied in the Oklahoma City Public Schools.

Value-Driven Schools

What drives a school, argues Thomas Sergiovanni, are the beliefs and values of staff—not its organization and administration. He maintains that traditional approaches to curriculum and management neglect the personal values of principals and staff. He describes an "amoeba theory" to make sense of the barriers to and opportunities for school reform.

Effective Schools

Daniel Levine and Eugene Eubanks describe the organizational arrangements and practices of several unusually effective secondary schools. Although three of the schools are in inner cities, they conclude that the changes implemented in them can help low achievers elsewhere. They go on to describe issues involved in major organizational reforms of schools.

Schools Within Schools

Mary Anne Raywid portrays four schools within one school: the Challenge Team, the Social Services Academy, Sequoia Institute, and Media. Though housed in one building, the schools are sufficiently separate and small to foster identification with their distinctive purposes. Each of Paradigm High's four programs features a unique ethos, extensive personalization, and an emphasis on the community of academic life.

A Restructured School

Joe Nathan describes lessons from an innovative K-12 school that appeared on the "Today Show" one month after it opened in 1971, and has since hosted 40,000 visitors. Exempted from many regulations, the school operates on the same budget as other district programs but insists that each student have an individual plan for learning; that the entire North American continent be used as a resource; that administrators teach; and that decision making be shared among students, staff, and parents.

Information-Age Schools

Is technology wasted on the schools? Robert St. Clair shows that unless principals rethink their roles, much of the enormous potential of computers and other modern technologies will be lost. Principals, he argues, must be aware of staff fears of substantial changes, and they must serve as role models in using educational technology if resistance to its applications is to be overcome.

Personalized Schools

Most students must adapt to uniform instruction. James Keefe asserts that all learning is personal, and instruction must be personalized for individual students. By employing a systematic cycle of diagnosis, prescription, instruction, and evaluation, schools can avoid teaching what students already know and what they are yet incapable of learning. Schools can ensure that all students can master essential knowledge but that the quicker students will not be held back by the slower.

A Computerized School

In the age of the computer, educators need to think of how computers may be effectively utilized to advance school objectives. Dustin Heuston describes the Waterford School that has employed a highly computerized curriculum in Provo, Utah, since 1981. Waterford has recently extended its grade structure from primary through secondary education at one site. The school has evolved considerably over the years; and the roles of the teacher and the computer have been reconsidered and modified. Heuston tells why and how.

A Late 21st Century School

Fenwick English takes us on a futuristic tour of school in the year 2088. He draws upon research on learning theory, computer technology, curriculum design, and socio-political theory to extrapolate from current trends the kind of school that our great grandchildren may enjoy. Surprisingly, however, all the innovations exist now in theory and within current technological frontiers.

Looking Ahead

Readers will see unique features in each of the real or envisioned schools described in the following chapters. Yet they will also see several common features.

Our analysis of the 12 organizational patterns suggests the several prevalent features detailed in the last chapter and shown in an analytic framework. These features may be found in as few as 5 and as many as 12 of the examples. The most common features in the framework are staff, parent and community involvement, principal leadership, change culture, curriculum alignment of teaching and testing, diversity, personalized learning, and skill mastery.

Readers may wish to employ the framework as an index of features exemplified in the 12 visions. They will be able to see how contributors have described the features they find attractive. Most of all, however, we hope that they will be stimulated to formulate a combination of features that best represents their own ideals for organizing learning toward the 21st century.

About the Authors

Herbert J. Walberg is a member of NASSP's Curriculum Council and Research Professor of Education at the University of Illinois at Chicago. He has advised education officials in the United States and eight other countries on educational productivity, and has often spoken and written on the subject of school reform.

John J. Lane is professor of educational administration and policy studies at De Paul University in Chicago. A former secondary school principal and director of instruction, he also served as national coordinator of Title V Programs for the U.S. Department of Health, Education, and Welfare.

Theodore R. Sizer is chair of the Department of Education at Brown University. Formerly dean of the Harvard Graduate School of Education, Sizer was author of the influential *Horace's Compromise*. He is chairman of the Coalition of Essential Schools.

William J. Bennett is president of the Madison Center in Washington, D.C. He was director of the National Humanities Center and chairman of the National Endowment for the Humanities. As U.S. Secretary of Education, he was known for his guest teaching in many schools and his emphasis on the American and Western heritages.

Arthur Steller is superintendent of the Oklahoma City (Okla.) Public Schools. He is a frequent contributor to professional journals and has recently completed a volume on effective schools.

Thomas J. Sergiovanni is Lillian Radford Professor of Education and Educational Administration at Trinity University, San Antonio, Tex. While his abiding research interests remain in the areas of leadership and motivation, his recent efforts have included work on effective schools and the principalship.

Daniel U. Levine is professor of educational administration at the University of Missouri-Kansas City. A former high school teacher in Chicago, he has conducted numerous studies dealing with urban education, compensatory education, school effectiveness, desegregation, and other topics, and has written textbooks in educational sociology and in the foundations of education. He currently serves as an adviser to school improvement projects in Kansas City and other school districts.

Eugene E. Eubanks is professor of education and urban affairs at the University of Missouri-Kansas City. A scholar and commentator on the issues of big city education and desegregation, his most recent writings have dealt with the effective organization of schools and the change process in the educational reform movement. A former mathematics teacher, principal, and deputy superintendent at the K-12 levels, he was dean of the school of education at UMKC for nine years.

Mary Anne Raywid is a professor of administration and policy studies at Hofstra University, where she also directs the Center for the Study of Educational Alternatives. A former high school teacher, she has been involved with educational reform efforts in the roles of policy advocate and analyst, evaluator, consultant, and resource person.

Joe Nathan is director of the Spring Hill Regional Issues Forum, Wayzata, Minn. He worked at the St. Paul Open School for seven years as teacher, program coordinator, and director of the Information/Training Program. A teacher and administrator in several public schools, he has written extensively about schools, learning, and leadership. Nathan coordinated the National Governors' Association project which produced *Time for Results: The Governors' 1991 Report on Education.*

Robert St. Clair is the immediate past president of NASSP. He served as a secondary school principal for the past 30 years, 26 of those years as a middle level principal in Hopkins, Minn. He contributed to *Developing a Mission Statement for the Middle Level School,* a publication from the NASSP Council on Middle Level Education.

James W. Keefe is director of research for the National Association of Secondary School Principals in Reston, Va. A former secondary school principal and a participant in NASSP's Model Schools Project, he also taught at the University of Southern California and Loyola Marymount University in Los Angeles. NASSP staff adviser to several Association task forces and standing committees, he is editor of the *Instructional Leadership Handbook*, and author of the Learning Style Profile.

Dustin H. Heuston is chairman of the Waterford Institute, Provo, Utah. After a brief career in banking, he was a college English teacher for eight years and then ran a private K-12 school, The Spence School, in New York City for eight years. In 1976, he founded the Waterford Institute, which has done extensive research in the use of computers in education. One of the activities of the Waterford Institute is running the Waterford School.

Fenwick W. English is professor and head, educational administration, at the University of Cincinnati. He was a superintendent of schools for five years in New York, and a partner in the international accounting and consulting firm of Peat, Marwick, Main, where he directed the North American elementary and secondary education practice for three years.

CHAPTER 1

Diverse Practice, Shared Ideas: The Essential School

THEODORE R. SIZER

NO TWO GOOD schools are ever quite alike. No good school is exactly the same from one year to the next. Good schools sensitively reflect their communities—both the students and teachers within the school building, and the wider neighborhood it serves. A good school respectfully accommodates the best of its neighborhood, not abjectly—playing whatever tune any particular special interest group might demand—but sensibly, balancing the claims of national values with those of the immediate community.

A good school is the special creation of its own faculty—its teachers, counselors, and administrators. These are its "permanent" folk. Students and their parents come and go, but a good school's core of veteran teachers and administrators make the difference. A school has character if its key faculty—its senators—feel collective responsibility for it, take its standards and its style seriously, and protect its reputation.

Such a commitment arises only when a faculty feels a sense of authority and control over its own school. Thus, just as a good school properly reflects its community, so too does it particularly show, and boldly, the convictions of its central staff, convictions that carry the authority of people who know that the school's reputation rests squarely on their judgment and strength.

If these conclusions about good schools hold—and they are widely shared among thoughtful school people and researchers who have looked carefully at successful schools—does this mean that there is no such thing as a good "model" school? The answer has to be yes: There is no such thing as a distinct, detailed blueprint for a fine school any more than there is such for a successful family.

But just as with families, while not exhibiting precisely similar configurations and traditions, good schools do share powerful guiding ideas, principles that are widely accepted even as they take different practical forms when a particular group of people in a particular setting shape them into day-to-day expectations and routines.

It is for this reason that the Coalition of Essential Schools has advanced its work as a set of commonly held principles rather than as a "model" for schools to emulate. The Coalition is, in effect, a process, an unfolding among a widely diverse group of schools of structures, routines, and commitments appropriate to each which are consistent with our shared principles.

There are precedents for this approach: the best known that of the group of schools in the Progressive Education Association's "Eight Year Study" of the 1930s and, more recently, the wide variety of Head Start programs that first sprang forth in the mid 1960s. The Coalition schools do not work in isolation, and they borrow from each other. The purpose of the collaboration is to spark a sustained conversation about what the commonly held ideas might mean and how a variety of communities might assist each other in finding their best practical expression. Coalitions give strength in numbers, fortitude at times of pressure. And for policy makers, a variety of schools provides a rich source from which ultimately to draw conclusions about the practical utility of the shared ideas.

The Coalition of Essential Schools rests on a simple set of "common principles." Most are stated in deliberately general terms. Most are very familiar, hoary old chestnuts of pedagogical commitment. Only two are specific, again deliberately so as provocations and restraints: no teacher in a Coalition school may have responsibility for more than 80 students; and the per pupil expenditure should not exceed that at comparable neighboring "traditional" high schools by more than 10 percent.

Only one of the common principles (the first) rests primarily on ideology—that of a democratic faith. It posits that in a democracy all citizens must be able to use their minds well, and must be able to function thoughtfully as critical patriots and effective members of the society, its communities, and work force.

The Nine Common Principles

The principles are as follows:

1. An Essential school should focus on helping adolescents learn to use their minds well. Schools should not attempt to be "comprehensive" if such a claim is made at the expense of the school's central intellectual purpose.

2. The school's goals should be simple: that each student master a limited number of essential skills and areas of knowledge. While these skills and areas will, to varying degrees, reflect the traditional academic disciplines, the program's design should be shaped by the intellectual and imaginative powers and competencies that students need, rather than by "subjects" as conventionally defined. The aphorism "less is more" should dominate. Curricular decisions should be guided by the aim of thorough student mastery and achievement rather than by an effort merely to "cover content."

3. The school's goals should apply to all students, although the means to these goals will vary as those students themselves vary. School practice should be tailor made to meet the needs of every group or class of adolescents.

4. Teaching and learning should be personalized to the maximum feasible extent. Efforts should be directed toward a goal that no teacher have direct responsibility for more than 80 students. To capitalize on personalization, decisions about the course of study, the use of students' and teachers' time, and the choice of teaching materials and specific pedagogies must be unreservedly placed in the hands of the principal and staff.

5. The governing practical metaphor of the school should be student-as-worker, rather than the more familiar metaphor of teacher-as-deliverer-of-instructional-services. A prominent pedagogy will be coaching, to provoke students to learn how to learn and thus to teach themselves.

6. Students entering secondary school studies should be those who can show competence in language and elementary mathematics. Students of traditional high school age but not yet at appropriate levels of competence to enter secondary school studies should be provided intensive remedial work to help them meet these standards. The diploma should be awarded upon a successful final demonstration of mastery for graduation—an "exhibition." This exhibition by the student of his or her grasp of the central skills and knowledge of the school's program may be jointly administered by the faculty and by higher authorities. The diploma is awarded when earned, so the school's program proceeds with no strict age grading and with no system of credits collected by time spent in class. The emphasis is on the students' demonstration that they can do important things.

The tone of the school should stress values of unanxious expectation ("I won't threaten you but I expect much of you"); of trust (until abused); and of decency (the values of fairness, generosity, and tolerance). Incentives appropriate to the school's particular students and teachers should be emphasized, and parents should be treated as essential collaborators.

8. The principal and teachers should perceive themselves as generalists first (teacher and scholars in general education), and specialists second (experts in one particular discipline). Staff should expect multiple obligations (teacher-counselor-manager), and demonstrate a sense of commitment to the entire school.

9. Ultimate administrative and budget targets should include, in addition to total student loads per teacher of 80 or fewer pupils, substantial time for collective planning by teachers, competitive salaries for staff,

and an ultimate per pupil cost not to exceed that at traditional schools by more than 10 percent. To accomplish this, administrative plans might include the phased reduction or elimination of some services now provided students in many traditional comprehensive secondary schools.

The Coalition of Essential Schools

Many schools have long reflected these principles in their practice. However, if these ideas are taken seriously—if they are followed with determination—many school routines, even ones of long and almost unquestioned status, must give way. What Seymour Sarason has aptly called the traditional "regularities" of school are seriously challenged by these principles.

Criticism is not enough. Coalition schools are moving beyond criticism to the development of new and more effective "regularities," ones which serve youngsters and teachers better by adhering more closely to accepted Coalition principles.

More than 50 middle and high schools have joined the Coalition since its formal inauguration in September 1984. Although all of these are still "in-the-making," many general observations about their efforts can now be expressed.

First, it is clear that the nine common principles necessarily act in combination. If one is pressed without the others, it will be smothered. Pushing hard toward a pedagogy of "student-as-worker," for example, inevitably affects the curriculum, which in turn affects the daily schedule. The synergistic quality of school practice so tellingly illumined by Sarason and others is readily evident in the work of our colleague schools.

Second, the significant and sustained support of the faculty is critical. In practice, this does not mean the enthusiastic embracing of all the Coalition ideas by every last faculty member. It does mean, however, that a significant and veteran minority of teachers, combined with the senior administrators at the school, must be committed to move ahead, even as other faculty usefully express their skepticism, by serving as "critical friends." The leadership of the faculty can neither be reluctant nor impatient. Reluctant folk make poor adventurers, and changing anything as complex and as commitment-charged as a school must be done carefully, slowly, and patiently. At the same time, it is clear that a few persistent saboteurs can demoralize and muffle the energy of any school.

Some Coalition schools started with a school-within-a-school pattern, an "Essential high school" as part of a larger unit. There are virtues in this approach, as it allows the small group of most committed teachers considerable freedom to move. Visible programs emerge quickly. However, hazards arise in the inevitable "we-they" character of the approach; Essential school-within-a-school teachers and students are inevitably compared with the rest, and jealousies emerge from real or imagined inequities.

Evolving a careful and necessarily long-range plan of "turning" a whole school on Coalition principles at once carries its own sorts of hazards. One is the invisibility of much progress—and politics likes quick, visible results. Another is the difficulty of taking into account the synergistic quality of the school; everything important affecting everything else makes turning a very large and complex high school exceedingly difficult.

Easiest of all, perhaps, is the founding of a brand new high school, a permanently free-standing institution with its own building, or an independent unit within a larger education complex of some kind. The founders can gather to themselves congenial colleagues as the school grows, and, if it is a school of choice, an equally congenial student and parent body. The debits of this approach are both the strain of starting an institution from scratch and the absence of traditions and rituals—those expectations which, when sensible, give steadying ballast to a school.

Third, the planning for a restructured program takes substantial, unremitting effort and emotional energy. Much planning by a significant core of the staff during summer months and during the academic year is necessary, and both time and arrangements for daily or at least weekly meetings of the key faculty are essential. Even the most carefully worked-through summer plan will need adjustment within weeks of being launched, and the time and personnel necessary for the continual assessment of progress and the changes it suggests must be built in. Most reformers outside the schools fail to recognize this need; there are well-intentioned "restructuring" efforts even today which provide no assistance either to the principal or the faculty of a school that wishes to try ambitious change.

Redesigning a school is one thing; the reshaping (retraining) of its faculty is quite another. Staff development (an ugly phrase, implying a passive, clay-like faculty) is critical. It must arise from the teachers' sense of their own need and must be planned over a substantial period of time. The traditional "one-shot-five-times-a-year" staff development days are a mockery compared with the work required for the redirection of teachers' and administrators' responsibilities (and attitudes) that serious restructuring requires.

Fourth, the Essential Schools movement is first and foremost a movement in *pedagogy*, in the relationship between teacher, student, and the subjects of study that bring them together. For example, the aphorism student-as-worker/ teacher-as-coach affects everything, from the way the school adheres to the expectations of both teachers and pupils to the nature and seriousness of staff development. Few recent efforts in school reform have started with the teacher-student-subject relationship, much less from pedagogy. Indeed, the importance of pedagogy is heard in few "reformist" quarters, and rarely from national commissions. The experience of Coalition schools that appear to be making progress, however, is already clear: Get the relationship of the youngster with the teacher right and subject matter and all else eventually will fall into place.

Fifth, the differences among youngsters, vaguely apparent to perceptive teachers, become clear when faculty-student ratios drop. Varying learning styles, differing motivations, rapid or sluggish rates of learning, and more all impinge on Coalition teachers. Getting the ratio down is one thing; using the practical possibility of serious personalization is a new prospect for many teachers—a happy luxury, but a troubling new responsibility.

Sixth, a school reform effort that arises from a set of *ideas* that a school faculty must carefully fashion into appropriate practical form—rather than a describable practice that is to be implemented—is an unfamiliar one in many communities. Accordingly, such an effort requires special political protection. School board members, superintendents, local business and political leaders, and the regional press all have their parts to play. The difficulties that Essential schools encounter do not end merely with the nature of the reform approach, but also in the inevitable clashes that arise from the setting of priorities by the Essential schools' planners. If thoroughness and the use of their minds by students is a truly serious goal, many traditional and usually pleasant school practices will have to give way.

Choices must be made, and some parties will inevitably be aggrieved. The politics of subtraction is the most difficult of politics, and the political supporters of Essential schools-in-the-making must be staunch and patient. This implies thorough understanding on the part of parents and other influential members of the community of what is being attempted. It demands that the school make the argument that the risk of doing nothing exceeds the risk of trying something new, that most "good" schools are not nearly good enough.

A final source of support is "critical friends," not only among the outsiders, but among colleagues in Coalition schools. Serious restructuring must be accompanied by a constructive peppering by knowledgeable people, friendly but persistently challenging. The very existence of these folks provides a running sort of accountability, and good allies. Their known presence strengthens the venturesome, and doubters both within the school and without are reassured that fair-minded critics are involved.

Seventh, Coalition teachers need great confidence in the subjects they teach. Often the compromise necessary to push the faculty/student ratios down is for teachers to work somewhat beyond their own specialties, with standards maintained by collaborative teams. For example, a humanities team is made up of teachers of English, social studies, fine arts, and foreign languages, with some members teaching several subjects. Quality control is maintained by specialists in each area. To teach somewhat outside one's field—sanding off the rust on one's English background if one is, say, an art teacher—takes self-confidence and a willingness to expose one's inadequacies to the critique of other teachers. This is often threatening.

The vigorous protestations against teaching out of area that one hears in many schools mask both the narrow preparation provided teachers in colleges and universities and a basic lack of scholarly self-confidence. (It always strikes me as odd that high school faculties insist on greater specialization than do, for example, graduate faculties of law or business. Is scholarly quality only calibrated by past formal study?) Schools in the Coalition have found that summer institutes are necessary to help teachers broaden and deepen their subject matter preparation. This priority must be reflected in any staff development plan.

Eighth, sustained and steady administrative leadership, particularly that of principals, is crucial. Coalition schools in communities where superintendents and principals have come and gone suffer intensely; in power vacuums the *status quo* flourishes. Constructive change requires leaders who have the vision and ability to assemble and hold teams of colleagues to the difficult task of trying to find a better way to school young people.

Finally, there must be a clear sense of the goals of an Essential school: the goals for the students, the teachers, the administrators, and the school as a whole. A prime vehicle to drive this goal-setting is the "exhibition," the demonstration by a student that he or she understands a rich core of subject matter and, equally important, can use it in resourceful, persuasive and imaginative ways. Few schools in recent years have ever tried clearly to articulate what students should be able *to do* to deserve their diplomas. We all tend to retreat into the familiar evasions—Carnegie units, seat time, and years of coverage.

No exercise can be more difficult for a faculty than that of addressing what the student should be able to do to deserve to graduate and none can be ultimately as liberating. Only by being clear about those general qualities that students must ultimately display can a faculty derive an educational plan, one that gives priority to helping the students achieve the identified strengths. Once wisely cast, such "exhibitions" can be the basis for sensible accountability, a measuring stick of quality that transcends the trivialization now reflected by our familiar quick-and-dirty, low-cost, paper-and-pencil tests.

Goals must be clear not only for students but also for the school as a whole. This requires a *plan*, one that details the necessary shifts in staffing, staff development, planning, the documentation of the project, and the resulting budget. Without a plan—even if it is creatively tentative, subject to constant revision—Essential schools will flounder. There is frustration enough in taking the common sense of the nine common principles into account without compounding it with vague direction.

The Coalition of Essential Schools promises no panacea, no quick model that can be put into place. It promises only an honest return to the basic questions about schooling, about growing up, about learning, and about teaching. It promises a hard, but ultimately liberating struggle for school folk, not only to forward their work in a setting that squares with the hunches of generations of successful teachers, but also to see youngsters—particularly those for whom traditional schools seem to have given up—perform in extraordinary ways.

The Coalition's Essential schools-in-the-making already signal promise in this regard. None of us wishes to make strident claims at this point, but we are convinced that when the basic ideas we share are rigorously adhered to, the world of schooling improves both for youngsters and for teachers.

The model of the Coalition school is, thus, not a generalizable model at all. Rather, it is an approach that leads to an idiosyncratic model for each community, a unique representation of what is best for that setting and its people and which is consistent with some powerful, old-fashioned ideas about learning and teaching. Patience, courage, and an endless sense of humor are required, but the promise is there, rich and increasingly visible.

Selected Readings

Goodlad, John. *A Place Called School*. New York: McGraw-Hill, 1983.

Grant, Gerald. *The World We Created at Hamilton High*. Cambridge, Mass.: Harvard University Press, 1988.

Hampel, Robert L. *The Last Little Citadel*. Boston: Houghton Mifflin, 1986.

Lightfoot, Sarah Lawrence. *The Good High School*. New York: Basic Books, 1983.

Sarason, Seymour. *The Culture of School and the Process of Change*. Boston: Allyn and Bacon, 1971.

Sizer, Theodore R. *Horace's Compromise: The Dilemma of the American High School*. Boston: Houghton Mifflin, 1984.

CHAPTER 2

James Madison High School

WILLIAM J. BENNETT

EDUCATIONAL EXPECTATIONS MUST be high, attainable, and worthwhile. This chapter is an attempt to add such substantive expectations to the graduation standards established in *A Nation at Risk*. Written with the advice of principals and teachers at a number of representative American schools, it is my idea of a sound secondary school core curriculum. It describes what four years of English and three years each of social studies, mathematics, and science should consist of. And it adds two years each of foreign language and physical education, and a half-year each of art and music, suggesting suitable content for them, and explaining why they should supplement the other required subjects.

This document should not be understood as an argument for the exclusion from high school curricula of special and vocational electives or substitutions. Indeed, in a number of places, it notes the value of elective classes for continued or supplemental study.

But schooling in the full set of core academic disciplines should be central to the true purpose of American secondary education, and consequently this curriculum is for the most part traditionally liberal and nonspecialized.

As James Madison wrote, "Knowledge will forever govern ignorance: And a people who mean to be their own Governors, must arm themselves with the power which knowledge gives."

In his honor, I call this core curriculum *James Madison High School*, and I think every American child deserves access to a secondary education like the one it describes.

In *First Lessons*, my report on American elementary education, I discussed the knowledge, skills, and habits of character toward which I thought the kindergarten through eighth grade curriculum should be directed. *James Madison High School* is in some sense a sequel to *First Lessons*, a vision of what good elementary education should prepare students for, and of how the ninth through twelfth grade curriculum can build on that foundation.

I should stress that *James Madison High School*, while reflecting the quality and character of a number of real-world models, is meant as a goal and an ideal, not as a monolithic program to be uniformly imposed or slavishly followed. Like *First Lessons*, *James Madison High School* is not a statement of federal policy. Nor can it be. The power to mandate a secondary school curriculum for American students does not belong to the federal government. Moreover, the Department of Education is specifically prohibited by statute from exercising direction, supervision, or control over the curriculum or program of instruction of any school or school system.

That is as it should be. We are a nation of local education policies and practices. And local schools must adapt to local circumstances. I do not presume to instruct school boards, administrators, principals, teachers, or parents in the precise shape, sequence, or specialized content of their secondary school curricula. They know best their own requirements and problems.

Instead, *James Madison High School* is simply a statement of my considered judgment on an important subject, an attempt to deal with a question I am often asked: How would you do it? What would you teach?

That seems to me a fair question, and one too important to duck or avoid. This document is my answer to that question, one that I hope will prove a useful contribution to the national conversation about education reform, suggesting directions for new attention and effort.

What Should Be Studied and Why It's Within Reach

Obviously, readers may demur from specific conclusions I reach in these pages. Different parents want different things for their children, and they want different schools to provide them. Still, I believe that there remains a common ground that virtually all our schools can reach and inhabit. And I believe that most Americans agree about where that common ground is—about what our students should learn.

We want our students—whatever their plans for the future—to take from high school a shared body of knowledge and skills, a common language of ideas, a common moral and intellectual discipline. We want them to know math and science, history and literature. We want them to know how to think for themselves, to respond to important questions, to solve problems, to pursue an argument, to defend a point of view, to understand its opposite, and to weigh alternatives. We want them to develop, through example and experience, those habits of mind and traits of character properly prized by our society. And we want them to be prepared for entry into the community of responsible adults.

Achieving these goals need not involve a curriculum of unrealistic intellectual pretensions. *James Madison High School* is a curriculum for the students we have, not for an imaginary class of teen-aged wizards. And it is also, I believe, the kind of basic program most Americans want for their schools. In my travels around the country, in my talks with teachers, principals, elected officials, and parents, I find that American opinion stands behind the kind of core curriculum *James Madison High School* describes.

In fact, programs embodying many of its features and principles are currently in effect at a number of schools around the country. "I am pleased to report that everything envisioned for *James Madison High School* is in place at (my school)," one principal wrote me. "We already use a curriculum similar to the one you propose," a Florida superintendent told us, "so I can certify to you that it works!"

Profiles of several excellent schools appear in this document. They are not alike in every detail. They serve inner-city and rural communities, suburbs and small towns. Their students come from comfortable and disadvantaged homes. Their graduates go on to further education or directly to work.

But what all these schools do share is a commitment to quality education—and to success. A broad, deep, and effective core curriculum is possible for almost all American secondary school students. I have seen it at work, producing measurable results, in high schools all over the United States. And I believe it is possible for virtually any school to refine and adopt a core curriculum similar to that which these schools provide so successfully.

To duplicate their success, some schools may need to eliminate the curricular clutter that *A Nation at Risk* decried. But even allowing for the nonacademic extras with which some states and localities burden their schools, a *James Madison High School* program (36 semester units of required work in grades 9-12) should not stretch most districts' capacities—or those of their students. There is plenty of room in the modern American high school for a strong and coherent basic curriculum.

Schools or localities bent on strengthening their requirements may fear shortages of qualified instructors for additional or improved classes. Clearly, *James Madison High School* affirms the need for American teachers who are fully in command of their subjects. In principle, we can ask no less of them. But no worthy statement of educational goals depends for its success on full and immediate implementation.

If we must reform and restructure our system of teacher training to provide the nation with enough men and women capable of teaching our students a solid core curriculum—and teaching it well—so be it. In the meantime, we may take heart from the example of a state such as New Jersey, which has successfully experimented with the alternative certification of teachers. There are, as it happens, a great number of adult Americans already able and eager to teach our students. We should take care not to perpetuate such unnecessary barriers to their employment as now exist in many states.

The bottom line is this: realizing curricular improvements may take work—new laws, better teaching, improved textbooks—but that does not make these improvements impossible, or any the less desirable. Indeed, they are a national imperative.

A Word About Student Differences

Any proposed core curriculum must acknowledge one reality above all others: among individuals, preparation for high school differs, as do intellectual ability and academic prowess. American students vary in ability, interest in learning, temperament, career aspirations, upbringing, family background, economic status, and racial and ethnic heritage. So how can a uniform and fairly demanding program like *James Madison High School* apply to the diverse student population of the United States? Will a rigorous academic program of high standards and expectations leave behind the less able and less advantaged?

Any serious answer to this question must begin by stipulating—and celebrating—the pluralism of American society. History shows that our pluralism has always posed formidable challenges to our schools. But history also demonstrates that for more than two centuries, American education has welcomed diversity, served classrooms full of the poor and the rich and the in-between, and often successfully bound them together in a cooperative undertaking. Today, still, every American child has an equal claim to a common future under common laws, enjoying common rights and charged with common responsibilities.

There follows the need for common education. In the past, American schools have proved that all children can learn and that scholastic excellence can transcend differences of race, religion, gender, and income. Our schools have refused to inflate or exalt such differences into permanent educational obstacles. And by their adherence to principles of true democratic education, our schools have given us millions upon millions of priceless gifts—educated citizens.

Today, however, there are some who view with disdain most efforts to restore and maintain high standards and high expectations, as if education reform were a mean-spirited trick to weed out weaker pupils before they get too far.

"We will have taken the high jump and raised it from five to six feet for a group of youngsters that couldn't jump five feet without extra help," one state school superintendent recently complained.

Americans should be wary of assertions like these. They may be expressed in the sweet language of concern, or they may be exhaustively footnoted with references to this or that conclusion of modern social science. Pessimism manufactures its own evidence. But at bottom, its message is always the same: "Some kids can't. Their color, class, or background will get in the way."

That's a discouraging message—and mostly a false one. In a previous Department publication, *Schools That Work: Educating Disadvantaged Children*, we documented the remarkable academic success of poor, disadvantaged, and minority children who, when given a chance at a solid education, take it—and learn. The fact is that while there may now be too many schools that fail to teach well, there is rarely anything "unteachable" about most of their students. Too many able and eager American students are not learning enough simply because of a mistaken belief that they cannot or will not learn.

Of course, our students are individuals, and so they present their schools with distinctive problems and needs and interests. There are below average and gifted students, there are students who speak English as a second language (or not at all), and there are students with learning disabilities and handicaps of varying kinds and severity. For these students, most local districts design particular classes or programs not treated here (Advanced Placement biology, remedial math, bilingual or special education, and so on). There will always be students who require extra attention; it should be available. And local authorities are best suited to devise and provide it.

These are questions of means, and they are important. Critics may claim that too few of our students are currently equipped to handle the curricular material described here in the time and form suggested. I believe otherwise. I think most American students could handle the classes in *James Madison High School*; again, I have seen students of all backgrounds do it.

There are, of course, some youngsters—too many, in fact—whose present preparation for high school is inadequate to the task. That is an argument for further improvements in elementary and intermediate education. It is not, however, an argument for abandoning any high school student in the present.

If one student—for whatever reason—cannot learn algebra and geometry in two years, then he should be given three, and the help he needs. But he should learn algebra and geometry. We may vary our pedagogy to achieve our educational goals, but we must jealously retain and guard those goals, the goals *James Madison High School* pursues: mastery of a common core of worthwhile knowledge, important skills, and sound ideals.

I've been told the following story: A teacher was visiting a high school classroom and speaking to a group of average and below-average students. They were talking about what their school should teach. The teacher asked these students what they wanted to study and what they wanted to read. One boy in back raised his hand. "We want to read what the smart kids read," he said.

That's the right answer. Responding to the needs and differences of individual students is a necessary but not sufficient mission for American education. Our schools cannot be governed by stereotypes associated with circumstance—stereotypes that encourage us to ask and expect too little from our students.

We in the United States have come a long way since Harvard president Charles William Eliot's 1908 recommendation that high schools teach different material to different students according to their "evident or probable destinies." Today, American schools must offer every child the curriculum he or she needs to find a *better* destiny. If we are serious about equal opportunity in school, I believe that *James Madison High School* is a curriculum for educational opportunity, and I believe access to a school that offers it should not be an accident of where a student lives or of how much money his or her parents make.

Some American secondary schools already resemble *James Madison High School*. Many others provide parts of it in their teaching and can reasonably be expected to provide the rest. Most of our students are ready; some are not. But we should do what can be done now; we should aim high not low, and remember that youngsters tend to perform according to our expectations of them. And we should look to a time when *James Madison High School* is more the rule of American education and less an exception.

The Program in Brief:
A Four-Year Plan

SUBJECT	1st YEAR	2nd YEAR	3rd YEAR	4th YEAR
ENGLISH	Introduction to Literature	American Literature	British Literature	Introduction to World Literature
SOCIAL STUDIES	Western Civilization	American History	Principles of American Democracy (1 sem.) and American Democracy & the World (1 sem.)	
MATHEMATICS	Three Years Required from Among the Following Courses: Algebra 1, Plane & Solid Geometry, Algebra II & Trigonometry, Statistics & Probability (1 sem.), Pre-Calculus (1 sem.), and Calculus AB or BC			
SCIENCE	Three Years Required from Among the Following Courses: Astronomy/Geology, Biology, Chemistry, and Physics or Principles of Technology			
FOREIGN LANGUAGE	Two Years Required in a Single Language from Among Offerings Determined by Local Jurisdictions			
PHYSICAL EDUCATION/ HEALTH	Physical Education/ Health 9	Physical Education/ Health 10		ELECTIVES
FINE ARTS	Art History (1 sem.) Music History (1 sem.)			

NOTE: This chart describes the *James Madison High School* curriculum. For each core subject it shows the number of years required and the names of courses that fulfill them. Each course is two semesters long, except as indicated.

In certain core subjects (English, social studies, and physical education/health), all students are obliged to take particular courses in a set sequence. In other core subjects (mathematics, science, foreign language, and fine arts), the selection of courses and/or their sequence is more flexible. This flexibility permits adjustments for individual student interests, needs, or abilities, and it provides room throughout the four-year program for elective, supplemental, or locally mandated study within or outside the seven core subjects.

The shaded area above represents room for such classes in a four-year schedule of seven-period days.

CHAPTER 3

Site-Managed Schools

JOHN J. LANE AND HERBERT J. WALBERG

IN JUNE 1985, the day after Chicago principal Dyanne Alexander issued several negative teacher ratings, most of her staff at Spencer School walked out. In June 1988, Alexander received the Chicago Business Association's Principal-of-the-Year Award. At the award ceremony, many of her former critics from Spencer School applauded. She is convinced that school-site management techniques made the difference.

When repeated requests to paint the dingy Spencer School corridors went unheeded by the central office, Assistant Principal Joseph Zielbauer coordinated a group of volunteers to come on a Saturday to do the job. For their efforts, he and the principal took considerable flack from trade unions and the central office.

Neither of these administrators was out to beat the system. But both subscribe to the principles of school-site management. They believe that to be effective, each school community needs to have some measure of control over its own destiny, or, as they might put it, "a fraction of the action." They are not alone.

Interest in school-site management or school-based governance is keen for several reasons. The political climate has spawned a variety of consumer-based movements and self-help groups. Site management, similarly, attempts to increase individual autonomy of stakeholders through shared information and expanded involvement in decision making.

Anti-bureaucratic sentiments also run high today—especially within large cities. The bigger-is-better philosophy prevalent among schools of the '60s no longer appeals. Parents' interests focus on the curricular offerings, leadership, and teaching in their neighborhood schools.

Research on educational effectiveness suggests that the individual school is a good locus for improvement. At a time when state legislators, community reform groups, parents, and unions vie for control of education, the individual school may be the best place to reconcile competing claims with local conditions and preferences.

Site Management

Essentially, site management is a form of decentralization that devolves planning, budgeting, and accountability to the site of the individual school. Site management appears to work best where the principal functions as chief executive officer working closely with staff, community, and a school advisory council composed largely of parents (Guthrie, 1986).

Site management does not imply that the school community makes all decisions on its own. On the contrary, site management attempts to strike a balance between school autonomy and central office control. Each may have distinct advantages and disadvantages.

Among the advantages of a centralized power are: uniform standards and coordinated decision making; unambiguous authority structures and consistent management operations; division of labor among specialists in curriculum, testing, and other fields; and cost savings resulting from elimination of duplicated services and activities. Central purchasing can often reduce unit costs. Centralized management, however, can lead to communication breakdowns resulting in ill-informed policies and autocratic management entrusted only to a few individuals.

Site-managed schools in decentralized districts can focus on a manageable scope of operations; they can vest decision making in those closest to the problem. These advantages come with a price—lack of uniform policies and poor logistical coordination among schools. Competition and rivalry among schools are a mixed blessing, depending on one's point of view.

Site management may better meet the desires of some principals, teachers, and parents who would serve together on a school council to formulate school practices. Some principals, for example, want more authority to appoint department heads and define their roles; to select, assign, coach, and evaluate the teaching staff; and to direct ancillary staff. Some teachers would like more control in the choice of textbooks, equipment, and other materials; the scheduling of classes; and the organization of the school calendar. Some parents and other community members would like a role in the allocation of financial resources and the selection and retention of the principal and staff members.

School councils operate within the constraints of district policies. The district office, for example, may continue to set broad educational goals and establish learning outcomes. School councils may select or invent approaches to achieve the district outcomes and their own visions.

The central office may continue to provide initial screening of teachers. But under site-level management, principals, in consultation with their school councils, may select teachers. Similarly, the office of business services may continue to purchase, warehouse, and distribute supplies to school buildings. But they may have to compete in convenience, quality, diversity, price, and speed with alternative vendors who supply directly to schools.

Site-level management may affect the central office in other ways. Central administrators may serve as arbitrators between individual schools and unions in labor contract disputes. Central office staff may need to establish computer networks or electronic bulletin boards to monitor school progress and to coordinate activities. It will probably be necessary for the central office to provide training, materials, and support during the transition from centralized to school-site management.

Developing an appropriate accountability system is a major challenge facing site-managed schools. It may be some time before a generalizable system is developed. Guthrie (1986) suggests that, at minimum, a school should be able to develop an annual report, prepared by the principal and the school council, that would be widely distributed throughout the community. The report might include: a statistical description of the school including enrollment projections, the number of teachers and their qualifications, student performance data, report summaries and research findings about parents and staff, a statement on future plans, and budget information.

Site Management in Chicago

When U.S. Secretary of Education William Bennett declared Chicago's "the worst schools in the nation," he frankly phrased what many parents, citizens, business people, and legislators had concluded. They felt that real reform would require that parents and community members be given a genuine voice in the operations of their schools, and a choice of public schools in which to enroll their children.

The plan, much of which is now enacted by the state legislature, is one of the boldest in urban education in this century. It relies on three ideas:

1. Local control through elected school councils
2. Division and assignment of powers to different governing bodies
3. Choice for parents.

Local control of schools is the norm, not the exception, in every Illinois district except Chicago. Nearly 750 of Illinois' 1,000 school districts serve fewer students than are served by the average Chicago high school. The division-of-powers idea, enshrined in our national Constitution, has worked well to limit centralized (often ignorant) power, and to devolve authority to small units that enhance local preference. Local choice in education prevailed in this country for 200 years before the advent of centralized public schools and compulsory attendance laws.

Under the new legislation, the present Chicago board will be disbanded to make a fresh start and to encourage greater citizen control. Mayor Eugene Sawyer will appoint a new board from a list of nominees prepared by a commission of parents and community members. The most important decisions will be made by elected school governing councils at the most devolved level—the individual school.

The councils, consisting of six parents, two community members, two school employees, and the principal, will control the school budget, have the power to hire and fire the principal, create a school improvement plan with the principal and teachers, and request waivers from the board to develop diversified experimental programs according to their local needs.

In what is known as one of the strongest union cities in the United States, teachers hired to fill new positions will be chosen on merit rather than seniority. Principals will be able to remove teachers 45 days after giving them notice of unsatisfactory performance if no improvement occurs. Principals will lose their tenure, but will be employed under three-year contracts controlled by the local school councils. For the first time, janitors, lunchroom managers, and other non-teaching staff will be under the principal's control, and must carry out "reasonable orders."

Central office spending will be cut by 25 percent in the first year, saving about $47 million to be reallocated to local schools. At least 50 percent of the cuts will come from central administrative positions. Federal and state funds for poor students will be spent in the schools they attend rather than for central office or systemwide uses. The Chicago School Oversight Authority of four mayoral and three gubernatorial appointees will evaluate progress and have the authority to discipline and dismiss central staff members and to monitor administrative spending.

Few decisions will be made by the central office, almost the opposite of the way the current school system is structured. Reversing the flow of power and responsibility, proponents believe, will restore opportunities for parental involvement in the schools, give principals and teachers a greater role in the day-to-day operation of their schools, and allow for substantial reductions in the size and cost of the bureaucracy. Skeptics doubt the ability of principals, teachers, and parents to reach informed, wise decisions.

In any case, persons aware of the experience with previous "decentralization" in New York City schools may mistakenly believe that the concept of school-based control is discredited. In fact, the reorganization in New York only moved power down to the subdistrict level, not to the school level. It merely created another layer of bureaucracy rather than radically devolving power to teachers, parents, and community members at the school site.

The Spencer School Revisited

Unlike many schools in Chicago that were not ready for this radical shift of authority, the Spencer School community of teachers, administrators, parents, and business representatives had tentatively answered several key questions during the past few years:

- What kind of school will best meet the needs of children in the neighborhood?
- What conditions must be changed to produce the top academic results?
- How can parents be constructively engaged?

- How can desirable practices be fitted into the constraints of state and district-mandated policies?

Discussion of such questions sensitized the Spencer community to many issues. The principal, teachers, parents, and community members were far more ready for the school council training programs than were many others who had not participated in the formulation of bold educational reforms.

No one could ensure that all would be well at the Spencer School nor at any of the other 600 public schools in Chicago. Feelings were widespread, nonetheless, that the Chicago Public Schools could not get much worse. Like other large-city systems, the Chicago schools suffer from a litany of problems: drug abuse, high dropout rates, burned out teachers, waste and inefficiency, poor educational methods, lack of parental involvement, and so on. But many Chicagoans and Illinois legislators believe that behind these symptoms is a shorter list of causes: centralized administration, a bureaucracy allowed to flourish, and lack of choice for both taxpayers and parents. To them, reform of urban education means fundamental reconstruction—not superficial refinements and small increments.

The children who enroll in the first grade in Chicago's public schools in the fall of 1989 are scheduled to graduate in the year 2001. The fondest hope is that the new legislation will improve their educational and life prospects. If their schools are successfully reconstructed, as most Chicagoans agree they should be, the educational experiences of these children will be enriched, and our metropolitan community will, in turn, be enriched by their greater productivity as adults.

References

Elmore, R. F. *Choice in Public Education*. Center for Policy Research in Education, Rand Corporation, 1986.

Guthrie, J. W. "School-Based Management: The Next Needed Education Reform." *Phi Delta Kappan* 4(1986):305-309.

Lane, J.J., and Walberg, H. J. *Effective School Leadership*. Berkeley, Calif.: McCutchan, 1987.

Stevenson, R. B. "Autonomy and Support: The Dual Needs of Urban High Schools." *Urban Education* 3(1987):366-386.

Walberg, H. J.; Bakalis, M. J.; Bast, J. L; and Baer, J. *We Can Rescue Our Children: The Cure for Chicago's Public School Crisis with Lessons for the Rest of America*. Ottawa, Ill.: Green Hill Publishers, 1988.

CHAPTER 4

One Model for Effective Educational Reform

ARTHUR STELLER

EDUCATORS ARE ENGULFED by school reforms. The excellence movement, the effective schools movement, legislative mandates, various reports and studies, teacher union demands for professionalism, and other similar pressures are as intense now as any forces ever affecting the American educational establishment.

A recent line from a state superintendent's speech was "Reforms, Reforms, Reforms! We are in reform school." There is a great deal of rhetoric. What is needed are practical, realistic approaches for accomplishing some of these lofty ideals.

Somewhat encouraging inclusions among the current crop of reforms are notions like team management, participative decision making, decentralization, and site-based management. For some reformers these ideas are considered means to give principals more authority and responsibility, while others suggest that it is teachers who should be more empowered.

Shifting the center of power often seems to be the primary emphasis of these school governance reforms. Whether a reform is top-down or bottom-up seems to be the most important consideration in some circles, rather than engendering student learning. Nevertheless, increased participation in educational decision making can lead to improved learner outcomes.

Many enlightened school administrators would like to involve more staff in decisions, but administrators are also confronted with the pressures of showing definite payoffs in learning. Consequently, they are reluctant to hand over the reins of power. The Model for Effective Educational Reform shown in Figure 1 takes that factor into consideration.

Rationale for the Model

The intent of this chapter is to offer one model for effective educational reform that incorporates top-down and bottom-up strategies while keeping the administrator in control of the process. The conceptual framework

Figure 1
A Model for Effective Educational Reform

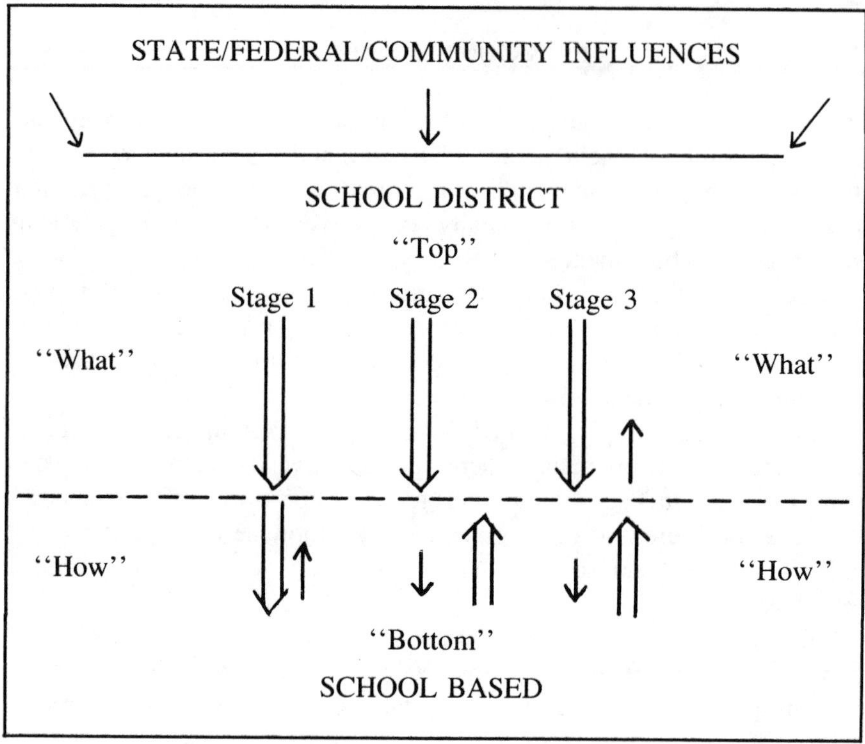

is succinct and relatively easy to grasp. Another useful feature of the model is that it includes the process for reaching the desired state—a balance between top-down and bottom-up influences as depicted at stage three.

The model is mainly designed for use by a superintendent in a school district. Principals, however, can employ the same framework by substituting "district" for "state/federal/community influences" and "classroom based" for "school based." The model can be applied generically, regardless of the relative position of the "top" and "bottom." A dynamic principal can reform a school using this model, but it is easier when all the schools in a district are working toward the same reform(s).

Principals at all levels are faced with the difficulties of bringing coherence to campus environments that are often only marginally connected internally. Any friction with the school district exacerbates the internal problems associated with realizing building goals, whether self-selected or imposed from outside. Schools are nested within districts and are limited by the boundaries of that outside environment.

Many researchers have concluded that the individual school is the appropriate unit for change. Educational change is usually measured in the school, simply because that is where the students are. To be effective, most changes must also physically take place in the school.

Typically, however, change actually begins in the central office with pilot studies, grant proposals, inservice programs, guest lecturers, mandates, and/or searches for a cooperative and willing principal. The folklore of school administration says that others should believe the innovation was their own idea. The myth is perpetuated while ignoring the reality that a high percentage of major educational changes—good and bad—come from outside the school. The top officials of a school district also have the capacity to stifle positive advancements and to restrain "off-the-wall" mutations that may come from school-based staff members. In fact, the superintendent, board members, and certain highly placed district administrators currently shape change in schools.

However, numerous exceptions to the rule exist. Some principals are leading the charge and leaping over recalcitrant district officials. Indeed, teachers and principals do need to make greater contributions to reform for the profession to keep advancing as it should. It is possible to point out these notable rarities and to promote more widespread participation, but the key to educational change resides within those who govern the school district. This may not be the way things should be, but it is the way they are. To effect change, the reformers, like the teacher, must begin where people are.

As the author constructed the Effective Educational Reform model to guide his way in the Oklahoma City Public Schools, he formulated other assumptions as well.

Underlying Assumptions

- Most successful and sustained major improvements in a school or district come from the top (or are at least strongly supported at that level).
- Increased student learning should be the product or byproduct of most major change efforts.
- Major changes regarding both what to do and how to specifically optimize learning schoolwide usually begin at the top of the organization (with the superintendent or principal).
- School-based staff members should be progressively more involved in shaping the means for implementing instructional programs.
- Continuous schoolwide renewal which positively affects learning at some point must involve both the top and bottom levels of the organization in direction setting and implementation.
- The effective schools research has produced a viable set of factors and

a focusing stratagem for use in a reform plan, with increased student achievement as the desired outcome.

- Significant change or reform that can be documented by enhanced student learning schoolwide or districtwide takes a minimum of three years, and more likely five years.

The remainder of this chapter briefly describes the model for effective educational reform and how one urban district is utilizing it from a top-down start toward a shared partnership. An effective schools project served as the basic content for this reform effort.

Model for Effective Educational Reform

The Model for Effective Educational Reform represents the overall approach employed in Oklahoma City to affect desired changes toward effective schools. A sampling of positive results will be offered to demonstrate the present level of success in reaching those ends. For a primary focus on raising student learning, the best indicator of progress is an upswing in standardized test scores. Across the district, all grade levels have improved their scores—some by as much as 15 percentile points in two years—with more than 3,000 students tested at each grade level. The gap between black and white student scores from third to fourth grade has been reduced by 13 percent from 1985-86 to 1986-87. The model provided the conceptual structure for organizing urban schools to actively pursue higher standards of student achievement.

State/Federal/Community Influence

The model begins with state/federal/community influences, since the educational reforms and regulations from these sources certainly affect organization for learning at school sites. These are often the ''givens'' around which school personnel must plan. The state is the predominant force in this arena; the federal government and the community exercise a lesser degree of influence. Some changes from these sources tell schools ''what'' to do in the form of goals or new courses; the ''how'' of implementation is even occasionally described in legislation. Neither schools nor districts operate without these constraints.

There have been numerous educational reforms at the state level in Oklahoma during the 1980s, many of which are prescriptive and definitive. The emphases have been on effective schools, teacher evaluations, North Central Accreditation, and statewide standardized testing. (At the same time, a huge drop in oil prices precipitated a tremendous downturn in the economy.)

Federal Chapter II funds were used to implement Oklahoma City's effective schools program. Locally, an equity oversight committee was established as an outgrowth of a desegregation plan. Equal opportunity and equal access for all students were initial concerns, but the focus evolved into equal outcomes. The effective schools program, with its objective of reducing gaps between the races, sexes, and socioeconomic groups, dovetailed with the community's concerns.

School District: Top-Down Reform

In this model, the main thrust for improvement originates from the top of the school district—the board of education, the superintendent, and the superintendent's immediate staff.

When the author came to Oklahoma City at the start of the 1985-86 school year, the school system was desperately in need of major reform. Principals and others wanted conditions to improve, but no agreement existed about what should occur. The board of education was dissatisfied, as were many patrons. Other citizens had become apathetic. There was a general lack of direction, and splinter groups were pulling in many directions.

This reform clearly came from the top—the state in the larger context, and the superintendent and board within the school district. A significant attempt was made to break the inertia, achieve some success, and expand leadership roles so that improvement and renewal would continue.

The leadership vision was boldly stated: "To be recognized locally, and in the state and nation, as a model urban school system." Six broad and supportive goals strongly suggestive of effective schools were approved and disseminated with the vision statement. A series of task forces were created to involve staff members in the development of programs to meet the goals.

Two of the more important goals were team management and effective schools. The latter spoke to interests at the state and community levels, while the former was intended to begin the transference of power necessary to reach stage three of the model.

STAGE ONE

In stage one, the schools were told what was to be accomplished and generally how it was to be done. Those who constitute the "bottom"—the school-based staff—were involved in the "how" of implementation, but to a lesser degree than district-level officials.

The vision statement and board goals were the reference points for what was to be accomplished. Each school, department, and administrator was required to develop goals and objectives that reinforced the board's goals.

The effective schools goal was a derivative of the top leadership's commitments. A task force of representative teachers, principals, and others was charged with identifying the best manner (how) to implement an effective schools approach, given a set of objectives and resource constraints. The task force selected the Kelwynn Group's videotape training modules and inservice program as a starting point.

According to this widely employed program, "School effectiveness is defined as a school where equally high portions of low and middle/high socioeconomic status children evidence mastery of the basic skills." Additionally, few group differences are evident in achievement according to sex or race. Both quality and equity are part of the definition.

The most commonly used factors or correlates of effective schools are:

1. Strong instructional leadership by the principal
2. Clear instructional focus
3. High expectations and standards
4. Safe and orderly climate
5. Frequent monitoring of student achievement.

Many school districts, including the one cited in this chapter, have added a sixth factor:

6. Active parental and community involvement.

Although individual participation was voluntary, every school was required to have a building-level cadre—the principal and four to five teachers—to train others at that campus. The building cadres were prepared by a districtwide group of administrators and teachers trained by consultants from the Kelwynn Group. Approximately 70 percent of the staff, including all the principals, completed this 36-hour program on instructional effectiveness.

In 1985-86, principals were told that they were expected to be instructional leaders (the "what"). For the next two years, they were often given concrete examples of how instructional leaders behaved. A variety of inservice programs helped to refine the assignment. Principals were organized into various committees, task forces, and other groups to share information and trade stories about how they functioned as instructional leaders. Several of these task forces took the specific behaviors associated with instructional leadership and incorporated them in the internship, selection, inservice, and evaluation procedures for principals.

The effective school correlates constituted a common theme throughout the district, tying together—for the first time—the curriculum and instructional program. Connections were established between the instructional program and other areas such as cocurricular activities and counseling. Some specific requirements were established for all schools: North Central Accreditation, school improvement committees for each site with 10 days of training by IDEA, and the establishment of an active PTA or PTSA.

Various districtwide efforts were begun to foster and support change at the individual school sites. For example, the curriculum and instruction division produced lists of essential skills, curriculum guides, and criterion-referenced test items for grades K-8. Textbooks were standardized throughout the district. Curriculum alignment projects were undertaken, correlating the curriculum objectives with texts and other materials, instructional methods, and assessment and evaluation measures.

The personnel department added items to job descriptions and evaluation instruments to reflect school effectiveness and other district directions. The research department produced statistical profiles, planning indicators, and disaggregated test data for school use.

These and other similar efforts were designed to give focus throughout the district on "what" instructional improvements were being promoted; give principals the tools (the "how") to maintain that focus within their buildings; and begin soliciting from the school-based staff ideas on "how" to best implement instructional improvements within their settings.

Stage Two

At this stage in the model, the district and school-based staff are rallying their collective energies around the central theme of the reform—effective schools. In actuality, no clear demarcation exists between stage one and stage two. What happens is that competent, enthusiastic school-based staff members take ownership of the reforms. The central office staff have trouble meeting school demands for more assistance. Increasingly, more classroom teachers and principals incorporate the instructional effectiveness techniques into their own repertoires. They become as expert in making these tactics work as the central office experts. More refinements and modifications in implementation come from the classroom than the conference room.

On the whole, the Oklahoma City Public Schools in 1988 are moving from stage one into stage two. Some individual elementary schools have already progressed to stage two in their improvement efforts. Many principals are at stage two, although their faculty members may be more identified with stage one. By the start of the 1989-90 school year, we anticipate that the majority of schools will be operating at stage two, with a few at stage three.

School-based staff members felt the brunt of stage one because they were the ones most required to change their behaviors. In stage two, district personnel must retreat from being overly directive and encourage teachers and principals to make more substantive applications. Central office supervisors must leave the details to teachers. This change can be unsettling for supervisors. New or struggling school building staff members should occupy the attention of district personnel who are uneasy about turning over responsibility.

Central office personnel, the superintendent, and the board must begin building the foundation for stage three during stage two. The first task for this group is to recognize that school-based staff must effect the actual implementation. This reality can be hard to accept, particularly for some board members. Just as difficult is to resist pressures from school staff members to prematurely determine the overall direction of the reform before mastering its processes. This is like the student telling the music teacher what songs he wants to play before mastering the prerequisite techniques.

Stage Three

At this stage, the superintendent, staff, and the board should be even less concerned with exactly how programs are implemented as long as the goals are achieved. They still retain control over what is done in the district. They focus mainly on the vision, the mission, and the goals of the organization.

For certain critical or high-priority areas, the "top" will continue to address how things should operate at the school level. The bottom and intermediate levels of the organization expand their responsibility for how implementation should proceed because they now are better able to contribute to what the school district is doing within the scope of the reform. The reception of new ideas at the top is now predicated on demonstrated school-based competence and an understanding of the reform by both the top and the bottom.

The school improvement programs established at each Oklahoma City school will be in full swing at stage three. With an emphasis on school-based management, these programs will involve the collaboration of patrons, school staff, students, administrators, and community members—all determining their school's future. A planning team of these key stakeholders will develop a long-range vision and then participate in a retreat to refine its vision and to establish school goals. A design task force will be formed to prepare detailed steps for initial improvements. More training, implementation, and maintenance will follow. As each year of improvement takes place, the next year is planned.

School improvement programs are part of Oklahoma City's team management system, which proposes that more and more staff throughout the district participate in making decisions that affect them. Currently at stage one, team management holds great promise as another successful reform approach. When team management reaches its potential in stage three, subsequent reforms should proceed with less friction and at a more guided pace.

Stage Four

While only three stages are outlined in this model, the author envisions a possible fourth stage. At this point, the local district will have reached a level of internal stability and outstanding success. The division of "top" and "bottom" will become less clear. Teachers will know more about the development of board policy and regularly contribute to what is undertaken. Likewise, the top will have the expertise and the credibility to suggest how, and often to have those ideas followed simply because of the efficacy of the proposal.

Stage four status will come through results—improved student test scores, staff awards, positive working conditions, and a harmonious atmosphere among all persons of the district. The state and the nation will recognize the school district as a lighthouse of educational excellence. Both the top and the bottom will push out of the encasement of state, federal, and community restraints. Politicians and scholars will ask the local district for advice. The district will exercise significant influence on outside forces.

Very few school districts will reach stage four, primarily because it will take 5 to 10 years of sustained effort—difficult to maintain in shifting political currents.

Problems

This model is heavy, initially, on top-down direction. Strong, knowledgeable leadership at the top is necessary to weather the inevitable resistance to change. Board members must be supportive. Those in opposition will claim employee morale is dropping and that professionalism is besmirched by canned programs and central office dictates. Ownership of the reform will take at least two to three years for school-based staff who do not see immediate results.

Constant vigilance must be exercised to ensure that district officials encourage initiatives from school-based staff. With success, there will remain a tendency to issue detailed how-to-do-it mandates from on high. Too often, the players at the top will change before the organization enters stage two.

Conclusion

A certain quick-fix mentality that simply does not square with the real world is inherent in many of the currently popular reform proposals. The principal can certainly set goals, establish priorities, arrange resources, and otherwise maneuver to arrive at a useful destination—in theory. It can even be true in actuality—so long as the principal also conforms to all federal regulations, state restrictions, board policies and initiatives, union contracts, and central office and superintendent interests. And, of course, the principal must keep students and parents happy in the process.

It is far more realistic to organize school reforms from the school district level and to start reform efforts from the top. Superintendents and school boards can utilize a process for moving toward a team or partnership approach for any proposed effort. Empowering school-based staff requires sensitivity at the top. Moving progressively toward shared decision making requires finesse and perseverance. A sudden shift to site-based management may guarantee instant publicity but not necessarily success for other reforms.

Certainly, the model presented here is not the only workable solution for meaningful school reform. Principals and school staff members can and should be active participants in any change that affects students, but there are simply too many schools and too many roadblocks for a school-by-school approach to have much of a long-term effect.

CHAPTER 5

Value-Driven Schools: The Amoeba Theory*

THOMAS J. SERGIOVANNI

THE BEST APPROACH to school organizational structure is a conservative one. This view does not mean abandoning efforts to improve the quality of life offered by schools to teachers and students, the curriculum, or existing patterns of planning, teaching, and evaluating. It does mean, however, that emphasizing drastic restructuring of present organizational patterns as the means to bring about significant improvements is neither practical nor necessary.

More important than the structure of the school itself is the undergirding theory of management and life, and the values, beliefs, and norms that constitute this theory.[1] How a school looks represents its outer structure; the values and beliefs that constitute its governing theory constitute its inner structure.

Changes in the former but not the latter reinforce the well-known adage, "The more things change, the more they stay the same." Although ideally inner and outer structure should change together, inner structural changes do not depend entirely on outer changes.

For these reasons, I will leave questions relating to how the curriculum is to be restructured, what should be the role of the department, and how schools might be better organized and reorganized to facilitate learning to others. Instead, I will propose five principles of "non-organization" that should be honored regardless of how one chooses to organize. The principles are as follows:

- Invert the rule
- Think amoeba
- Emphasize sense and meaning
- Build with canvas
- Remember moral aspects of leadership.

---

1. For an elaboration of the ideas presented in this chapter, see T. J. Sergiovanni, *The Principalship: A Reflective Practice Perspective*. Boston: Allyn and Bacon, 1987.

Invert the Rule

Standard theories of management and leadership assume that schools and other enterprises are managerially tight and culturally loose. They portray the operations of schools as resembling the mechanical workings of a clock composed of cogs and gears, wheels, drives, and pins, all tightly connected in an orderly and predictable manner. It follows from this tidy and orderly clockwork view that the task of management and organization is to gain control and regulate the master wheel and master pin.

Sometimes the master wheel and pin take the form of a new curriculum, a sophisticated testing program, a design for monitoring what teachers do and for evaluating their teaching behaviors, a program that trains teachers to implement a specific teaching model, or a new grouping pattern that requires teachers to teach differently. It is assumed that if one gains control of the master wheel and pin, all the other wheels and pins will move responsively and the leader's intents will be accomplished.

Teachers, for example, will teach the way they are supposed to and students will be taught what they are supposed to learn. Unfortunately (as the classic Hawthorne studies and dozens of others since have clearly demonstrated), this rarely happens—at least not on a sustained and continuous basis, and not without excessive and regressive monitoring and other enforcement efforts.

Successful improvements in schools require that we invert this rule. Schools are not managerially tight and culturally loose, but rather are culturally tight and managerially loose. The reality is that teachers and other school workers respond much more to their values and beliefs, how they are socialized, and the norms of the work group than they do to management controls.

Organizational designs and structure proposed for the high school that ignore the inverse rule will not be accepted. Designs and structures now in place or forced into place that ignore the inverse rule will not be implemented. If changes do not affect the teaching and learning that takes place behind the closed classroom door, they can hardly be considered changes.

Think Amoeba

The rule "managerially tight and culturally loose" forces us to think rationalistically about the world of schooling and administration rather than rationally. The first requirement of a rational theory of administrative practice is that it be practical and realistic. Theories in educational administration must fit the way the world of schooling works. If they sound logical and make excellent copy for books and articles but don't fit, they are not rational, but rationalistic.

Thinking amoeba, for example, is a rational approach to understanding the nature of administrative work. Running a school is like trying to get a giant amoeba to move from one side of the street to another. As the "glob" slips off the curb onto the street and begins its meandering journey, the job of the administrator is to figure out how to keep it together while trying to move it in the general direction of the other side. This involves pulling here, pushing there, patching holes, supporting thin parts, and breaking up logjams.

The pace is fast and furious as the administrator moves first here, then there. Throughout, the administrator is never quite sure where the glob will wind up, but never loses sight of the overall goal of getting it to the other side. Mind, heart, and hand become one as the administrator "plays" the glob, relying on her or his nose for globbiness, and ability to discern and anticipate patterns of movement that emerge.

How different is this view from the one offered in the literature—a view that would have us attempt the crossing of the street by first specifying our destination as a highly specific outcome and then implementing an explicit, linear, and managerial chain of planning, organizing, directing, controlling, and evaluating as if contexts were fixed and people were inanimate. This simplistic pattern might be rational for running a railroad but is rationalistic when applied to running a school.

Whatever our aspirations and plans for school improvement, they must reflect the amoeba-like characteristics of schools. "Think amoeba" might not be tidy advice, but it is practical advice.

Emphasize Sense and Meaning

One might reasonably ask, "But are not ideas like 'think amoeba' and 'managerially loose, culturally tight' nonleadership views of school improvement?"

They are indeed non-organizational views of school improvement, but they are not nonleadership views. If what matters most to teachers are values and beliefs, patterns of socialization, and norms that emerge in the school, then these are the characteristics that must be considered as key to school improvement efforts. These characteristics fall within the domain of leadership. As leadership is practiced in an amoeba-like and structurally loose world, some things matter more than others.

For example, whether leaders are warm or cold in personality, more likely to use Style A than B, tall or short, skilled at dressing for success or not, count much less than what leaders stand for, and their ability to communicate ideas and meanings in a manner that inspires, is compelling, and makes the work lives of others more significant. Such concepts as purposing and working to build a shared covenant that bonds people together in pursuit of common values become important. Symbolic and cultural leadership are considered key leadership forces.

The conventional wisdom with respect to work motivation and increased performance is that "what gets rewarded gets done." In practice, this truth takes the form of leadership bartering, as principals trade something they have for something they want and it works. But leadership by bartering has its limits, too. It results in calculated involvement from people. One complies as long as the exchange continues. When you are no longer getting what you want, you no longer give in return.

On the other hand, when principals emphasize purposing and covenants, practice takes the form of leadership by bonding. Here, the task of the leader is to create a moral order that bonds both leader and followers to a set of shared values and beliefs. A new wisdom with respect to work motivation and increased performance emerges: "What is rewarding gets done," and it gets done even when the principal isn't looking, monitoring, or otherwise checking.

The power of calculated involvement pales when compared with moral involvement. Symbols and culture become important concepts in bonding leadership as values are communicated and agreements are struck. People become believers in the school as an ideological system. They view themselves as members of a strong culture that provides them with a sense of personal importance and significance and work meaningfulness. The result is increased intrinsic satisfaction and greater motivation.

Build with Canvas

The latest innovation in U.S. military technology is a line of folding tanks constructed of canvas and designed to serve as decoys on the one hand and to create an illusion of strength on the other. Building with canvas is not a bad idea when tinkering with the structure of schooling. For example, one well-established principle in the organization literature is that "form should follow function." Otherwise, the ominous corollary, "if form does not follow function, then function will be modified and shaped to fit the form" will become a reality. "Form should follow function" is good advice and the danger of the corollary (bureaucratizing curriculum, teaching, and supervision to fit the school's bureaucratic organization) is well known and widespread. We seem not to make much headway in avoiding the corollary because we try too hard to follow the principle. The principle is not realistic, and the corollary wins by default. The way out of this dilemma is to build with canvas.

Schools have multiple and often conflicting purposes that make exact alignment of structure and purpose difficult if not impossible. Perhaps a better approach would be to seek balance among competing requirements when thinking about how best to organize and structure. Three competing requirements that should be considered are legitimacy, efficiency, and effectiveness.

When organizing for *legitimacy,* schools are responding to the demands and pressures they face from external audiences such as school boards, local community and professional groups, and state accrediting agencies. These audiences require that schools look the way they are "supposed to." To obtain legitimacy, the school must be able to communicate to its audience a feeling of competence. In return, it receives needed statements of confidence.

Schools, for example, must be viewed as well managed, orderly, and safe; adults must be perceived as being in control; events must run smoothly. The general flow of schooling must be viewed as familiar to audiences, and this often means not being perceived as too innovative or otherwise too out of pattern. Further, state requirements and legal mandates must be met. However one chooses to operate with respect to the inner structure of schooling, these outer structure requirements will need attention.

Organizing for *efficiency* recognizes that schools are characterized by limited time, dollars, and human resources. Limited resources must be distributed in a fashion that serves the most common good. Tutorials, for example, may be effective ways to organize for teaching, but on a large scale may not be efficient, given our commitment to mass education and our staffing patterns of between 20 and 30 students per teacher.

By instilling the value of collegiality among teachers and encouraging flexibility for informal shared teaching, the tutorial concept can be used without the risk of creating and institutionalizing a new organizational structure. Efficiency is an important consideration as school organizational structures are determined. Whatever pattern of organization is chosen, if it does not look efficient, it will not be accepted.

Organizing for *effectiveness* reflects a concern for doing the job of teaching and learning according to agreed-upon specifications and in a manner that reflects competence. Schools are expected, for example, to have a specific curriculum in place, to have definite goals and objectives, and to organize themselves for effective evaluation. Further, certain criteria for schooling considered important by state education departments, regional accrediting agencies, and local educational experts dictate fairly specific organizational and structural requirements.

Because of their relative remoteness, external audiences are attracted to the general features of school organizational structure rather than to the details of how these features are to be interpreted and articulated in the day-by-day processes of schooling. Thus, schools are able to exercise a surprising amount of freedom as they interpret policies and rules and implement organizational designs in ways that support sensible teaching and learning.

If schools build in canvas, they are able to provide the right public face. This gives them the freedom to interpret, decide, and function in ways that make sense. The more effective they are in communicating the right flow of images to external audiences, the freer they are to interpret structures and designs meaningfully for teachers and students, and for learning.

In sum, administrative work resembles an amoeba crossing, and the world of schooling is culturally tight and managerially loose. Practice must reflect these realities if it is going to work. But to have the legitimacy and freedom to practice, one needs to create the illusion that the school is being run like a railroad. For this reason, we need to build with canvas.

Remember Moral Aspects of Leadership

Creating illusions and building with canvas raise obvious moral questions in the minds of those not versed in the nature of amoeba crossings. Such ideas are deceptive, one might argue, and have no place in the lexicon of administration. Moral questions are not raised by being sensitive to such human realities as loose connectedness, competing preferences and interests, socially constructed reality, and the importance of norms and values. They are raised, however, when we ignore these realities by continuing to push an ill-fitting, rationalistic management theory. The consequence of this latter strategy is the constant attempt to shape human nature to fit theory. A more moral and rational strategy would be to use a theory as the basis for school improvement that fits human nature better in the first place.

Moral questions loom large, nevertheless, as we seek to bring about school changes. Whenever there is an unequal distribution of power between two people, the relationship becomes a moral one. Leadership involves an offer to control. The follower accepts this offer on the assumption that control will not be exploited.

In this sense, leadership is not a right but a responsibility. Its purpose is not to enhance the leader, but rather the enterprise. Leaders administer to the needs of their enterprise by being of service and providing help. The test of moral leadership is whether the competence, well-being, and independence of the follower is enhanced as a result of accepting control; whether the enterprise of which both leader and follower are a part benefits.

Leadership combines management know-how with values and ethics. Leadership practice, as a result, is always concerned both with what is effective and what is good; what works and what makes sense; doing things right and doing right things. As school improvement projects are considered and as new organizational designs are being implemented, questions of what is good, what makes sense, and what is worth doing deserve equal billing with questions of effectiveness and efficiency.

When the two sides of the ledger are in conflict, leaders will be known by the side they emphasize.

Most of the emphasis in discussions of leadership and authority is given to a person's expertise, credentials, position in the organization, and interpersonal style. These are, of course, important sources of authority for the principal, but rarely are they enough to carry the day in bringing about school improvement.

The problem is that these sources are secular. They seek a response from the human mind and hand. But the unique human response is one of spirit, and our spirit responds to values, beliefs, moral dimensions, and standards. It is the character of leadership that taps the spirit. How credible is the leader? Is the leader honest, forthright, and sincere? Does the leader model beliefs, live purposes, exemplify standards? In essence, what does the leader represent, and does this representation symbolize something of value to followers? When symbolic leadership is emphasized, then the other sources of authority take on moral characteristics.

"It is in and through symbols that man, consciously or unconsciously, lives, works and has his meaning." (Thomas Carlyle)

Assumptions Underlying the Amoeba Theory

Theories of management and leadership are based on different, albeit often implicit, images of human rationality. When a principal chooses a theory from which to practice a particular image of rationality, it is assumed to fit the real world. A better fit between theory and practice will occur by starting the other way around. Choose the image of rationality that fits the real world first and then find a theory that fits the image.

Three images of human rationality are briefly described below (Shulman, 1988). All three are true to a certain extent, but some are thought to be "more true" than others.

1. Humans are rational; they think and act in a manner consistent with their goals, their self-interest, and what they have been rewarded for. If you wish them to behave in a given way, make the desired behavior clear to them and make it worth their while to engage in it.
2. Humans are limited in their rationality; they can make sense of only a small piece of the world at a time, and they strive to act reasonably with respect to their limited grasp of facts and alternatives. They must, therefore, construct conceptions or definitions of situations rather than passively accept what is presented to them. If you wish them to change, engage them in active problem solving and judgment. Don't just tell them what to do.
3. Humans are rational only when acting together; since individual reason is so limited, men and women find opportunities to work jointly on important problems, achieving through joint effort what individual reason and capacity could never accomplish. If you want them to change, de-

velop ways in which they can engage in the change process jointly with peers.

The first image—that humans are rational—fits the railroad theory of management very well. The second and third images, by contrast, are better accommodated by the amoeba theory. Instead of an engineer who drives the train on a scheduled and fixed path to an explicit destination, the principal serves as the nucleus of a cell seeking to bring order, definition, and direction to a mass of protoplasm whose path would otherwise be willy nilly.

Rationality is achieved by helping people to make sense of their world. As sense builds, limits on rationality are overcome. Sense builds when people are able to construct their own definitions of situations and are involved with the leader in active problem solving. The limits, however, are too great for anyone to go it alone. Thus, one key strategy for sense building is the pooling of human resources in an effort that expands individual reason and capacity to function.

When running the school as a railroad, it is important to emphasize (in order) ends, ways, and means. First, establish your objectives. Then, given your objectives, develop a plan that includes the proper management protocols for obtaining the objectives. Next, marshal your human resources. Prepare them carefully by providing the necessary expectations and direction, appropriate training and development, and the psychological support that will allow teachers and administrators to undertake assigned responsibility with motivation and commitment.

Ends, ways, and means assume a certain predictability, stability, and rationality that does not exist in the real world of schooling. Further, this view of planning places too much of the burden for school success on the principal. It becomes the principal's job to set the system up, command compliance, and provide the necessary controls to ensure compliance. Should things not work out as intended, the principal must be held accountable, not teachers, parents, or students.

Unfortunately, because of the rational management biases that exist in our society, the ends, ways, and means system must be in place in the school. But it behooves the principal to build this system with canvas rather than stone. A canvas system does not serve as a model for action, but as a source of legitimacy from a public that expects the school to look a certain way.

When moving the school as amoeba, one needs to plan in reverse. Without losing sight of the overall vision for the school, the principal first emphasizes means, then moves to ways, and finally to ends. As Hayes (1985) points out, "An organization that takes a means-ways-ends approach to strategic planning assumes everybody is responsible for its prosperity. Its success rests on its ability to exploit opportunities as they arise, on its ingenuity, and on its capacity to learn, on its determination and persistence.'' The emphasis in means, ways, ends is on the development of people, on building their talents and commitments, on linking them to colleagues so that together they are able to accomplish more than alone, on encouraging their minds and hearts and helping their hands.

Once human resources are built up in both skill and heart, then the school is better able to acquire and develop new and better ways to function, to create opportunities, and to exploit circumstances in a manner that results in more effective school performance. Because of the unpredictability of the world and the limits of human rationality, it makes sense to emphasize building capabilities of people first, encouraging them to develop the ways and means for using their capabilities, than it does to develop plans and then seek the know-how and commitment to implement the plans.

Testing the Amoeba Theory

Let's put the amoeba theory and the other principles of nonorganization described here to a test.

You have worked with many leaders during the course of your career. Begin by thinking about as many leaders as you can. Let them pass through your mind as if you were flipping through the pages of your leadership experiences catalog. Some of the experiences will bring to mind leaders you remember as having been very successful, others as having been unsuccessful, and still other leaders who seemed to have an indifferent effect.

1. Select the most successful leader you have ever personally encountered. This leader may have:
   - Inspired your spirit and interest
   - Motivated you to work harder and perform better
   - Increased your commitment and belief.
     a. How would you describe this person's leadership style?
     b. How would you describe this person's ''theory'' or ''philosophy'' of management and leadership?
     c. Give one concrete example that illustrates this person's approach to leadership. (For example, what was the issue? What did the leader do? What were the consequences?)

2. Select the least successful leader you have ever personally encountered. This leader may have:
   - Deflated your spirit and interest
   - Caused you to work less and your performance suffered
   - Increased your alienation and disbelief.
     a. How would you describe this person's leadership style?
     b. How would you describe this person's ''theory'' or ''philosophy'' of management and leadership?

c. Give one concrete example that illustrates this person's approach to leadership. (For example, what was the issue? What did the leader do? What were the consequences?)

3. Select a leader you personally encountered who would be a prime example of a "nonsuccessful" leader (neither successful nor unsuccessful). This leader may have:
   - Bred indifference with respect to your spirit and interest
   - Had a nonmotivational effect in the sense that you did what was expected but nothing else
   - Bred indifference with respect to your commitment and belief.

   a. How would you describe this person's leadership style?
   b. How would you describe this person's theory or philosophy of management and leadership?
   c. Give one concrete example that illustrates this person's approach to leadership. (For example, what was the issue? What did the leader do? What were the consequences?)

For our purposes, ignore the least successful leader you encountered, focusing instead on the most successful and nonsuccessful leader. If the theory of management and leadership I propose fits the principalship better than its inverse, the successful leader you recalled will resemble the nucleus of an amoeba, and the nonsuccessful leader a railroad engineer. If I am wrong, then it will be the other way around.

References

Hayes, Robert H. "Strategic Planning—Forward in Reverse?" *Harvard Business Review*, November-December 1985, pp. 111-119.

Shulman, Lee S. "Teaching Alone, Learning Together: Needed Agendas for the New Reforms." In *Schooling for Tomorrow: Directing Reforms to Issues that Count*, edited by Thomas J. Sergiovanni and John H. Moore. Boston: Allyn and Bacon, 1988.

CHAPTER 6

Organizational Arrangements at Effective Secondary Schools

DANIEL U. LEVINE AND EUGENE E. EUBANKS

OUR MAJOR CONCERN in this chapter is the restructuring of secondary schools in order to provide more effective organizational arrangements and to ensure substantial improvement in student performance. In using the term "organizational arrangements," we will be referring primarily to policies and practices involving the assignment of teachers and students to learning units and decisions concerning the organization and delivery of curriculum.

Since effectiveness in organizational arrangements depends on their compatibility and coordination with other major aspects of school operation such as staffing policies, student evaluation, and discipline practices, we necessarily will also be concerned with how various policies and practices function together to constitute an effective organizational structure.

Examples of Successful Restructuring

Our selection of examples for this section is not meant to imply that the schools and approaches we describe are the only ones that have been or are likely to be successful. Just the opposite, we believe that the precise nature and mixture of organizational arrangements and related practices which are most likely to be effective at a given school depend to a considerable extent on its history, current problems, faculty and student composition, unique mixture of priorities, and other idiosyncratic considerations that vary from one location to another.

On the other hand, we are convinced that relatively few secondary schools have been unusually successful in producing levels of achievement much higher than can be found in most other schools with a similar socioeconomic mixture of students, perhaps in large measure because few secondary schools have been substantially restructured to improve their organizational arrangements.

In addition, we will concentrate on schools about which we have some first-hand knowledge, since we are relatively confident that improvements reported at these schools really have been registered at some point in their recent history.

South Boston High School

Substantial improvements in school functioning and student performance were achieved at South Boston High School after a new administrative team (including Jerome Winegar and Geraldine Kozberg) was appointed in the late 1970s. Among the interrelated developments that helped produce large improvements in reading achievement, attendance, and postsecondary enrollment were the following (Kozberg and Winegar, 1981):

- Most ninth and tenth graders were placed in reading and writing courses rather than in traditional English classes, and methods used to teach reading and writing were drawn from theory and research about learning among disadvantaged adolescents.[1] The average ninth-grade reading score among South Boston's economically disadvantaged population increased from the sixteenth percentile in 1979 to the fortieth percentile in 1980, and the tenth-grade average increased from the eighteenth to the thirty-second percentile.
- A number of in-school and out-of-school alternatives were initiated to address the learning problems and preferences of students. These alternatives included a self-contained school-within-a-school emphasizing academic learning, a mini-school emphasizing experiential learning and individualized instruction, and a Transportation Learning Center.
- More than two-thirds of the incumbent faculty members were replaced by teachers willing to discard traditional methods and practices that had been largely ineffective.
- Students were placed in high school mathematics courses rather than in "business mathematics" that actually repeated beginning arithmetic.
- Work-study programs based on learning opportunities in the community were made available to many students after the ninth grade. Paid work-study assignments were concentrated at selected sites such as Boston City Hospital, and participating students received coordinated instruction from the academic staff and the work-study staff. Beginning work-study experience in the tenth grade and coordinating academic and vocational instruction proved highly motivating for students who previously had been alienated from school.
- Discipline was firm but fair. Stricter attendance and tardiness policies were introduced with the assistance of parents, the Student Council, and community representatives.

---

1. A 1987 summary of research conducted by the Project on Adolescent Literacy indicates that such methods include emphasis on students' experience in actually reading and writing, instruction in comprehension-development strategies, and integration of reading, writing, speaking, and listening activities.

- Strong security measures were imposed, as needed, to ensure the safety of students. Measures included the appointment of a youth-oriented security patrol and the partitioning off of dangerous locations.
- Systematic guidance in learning and personal development was emphasized for both ninth and tenth grade students, in part through a required career exploration course in the ninth grade. To provide structured assistance for ninth graders, youth-oriented personnel were selected to serve as homeroom teachers, and ninth grade support groups were established. In addition, the fact that South Boston is a relatively small school allowed all administrators and counselors to know every student by name.

Washington High School

Changes comparable to those at South Boston have taken place at George Washington Preparatory High School, located in an inner-city community in Los Angeles. Following the appointment of a new principal (George McKenna) in the late 1970s, student achievement and the percentage of graduates going on to college increased substantially, and the daily absence rate fell from 33 percent in 1979-80 to less than 10 percent in 1985-86.

The actions and changes that appear to have helped in bringing about these improvements include the following (U.S. Department of Education, 1987):

- Remedial and tutoring programs were established in all subject areas; students receiving a D or F were required to attend Saturday sessions.
- "Magnet centers" in mathematics, science, and communications were formed, with small classes and extra help for students in college-prep courses.
- Parents and students were required to sign a contract in which students promised to obey school rules, adhere to a dress code, and complete all assignments.
- Nearly 85 percent of the faculty were replaced by new teachers willing and able to implement changes in organization and instruction.
- Parents played an active part in monitoring student attendance.
- Teachers were required to assign homework and visit the homes of absentees.
- Strict discipline was enforced, frequent "hall sweeps" apprehended students not in class, and anti-graffiti squads of students were organized.

Wingate High School

Impressive gains in student motivation and performance also have been attained at George W. Wingate High School in Brooklyn, N.Y. Wingate, like many other inner-city secondary schools enrolling mostly poverty-level students, showed achievements that were abysmally, even disgracefully, low.

Comprehensive changes were initiated by Principal Robert Schain and his colleagues in the late 1970s (Schain, 1980):

- Emphasis was placed on development of reading and language abilities, including creation of a basic skills mini-school, a corrective reading program, after-school reading clinics, and a schoolwide program for teaching reading and writing in all classes.
- A school-within-a-school (the Alpha Program) was established for high-risk students. It featured special concentrations of courses in medical science flight training, labor studies, behavioral science, television and radio, commercial art, house construction, police science, and other areas.
- The importance of providing counseling and health services and information for students was stressed.
- Wingate's intensive, comprehensive, and ongoing staff development program counseled and encouraged many faculty members to leave. Others were recruited and trained to provide instructional support and leadership in line with the school's priorities.

Dewey High School

The three schools cited above are inner-city schools with predominantly working-class enrollments. In contrast, John Dewey High School has a diverse student body representing a cross-section of Brooklyn. Established in a new building in 1969, Dewey appears to have had considerable success in improving student motivation and behavior, facilitating learning, and increasing the levels of student performance.

Major aspects of the organizational and instructional arrangements that contributed to these outcomes included the following (Levine, 1971):

- A longer school day for both teachers and students was scheduled to accommodate Dewey's ambitious goals for student learning.
- Basic academic classes were reorganized. Students needing significant assistance could enroll in smaller classes made possible by the redirection of high achieving students to elective mini-courses with academic credit. For example, the English department offered mini-courses in Introduction to the Novel, The Bible as Literature, Literature of Protest, and many other themes to students who demonstrated mastery in basic English.
- Blocks of academic elective courses were scheduled so that students could major in broad areas such as law, health, technology, and foreign languages.
- Fifty percent of the faculty was selected by the principal without regard to seniority as part of an agreement with the United Federation of Teachers.

- Based in part on intensive faculty planning during the longer school day and also the year before Dewey opened, independent learning centers were established for each academic department. Students worked and/or were tested at the centers to obtain credit for mastering material in Dewey Independent Study Kits (DISKS) prepared by the staff.
- Students were assigned to a single guidance counselor for their entire school career to provide support for the independent learning.
- A program was established for upper-grade students to spend one day each week in supervised learning assignments in the community. Assignments undertaken in this program included work in marine biology at the Coney Island Aquarium, the study of anthropology at the Museum of Natural History, and serving as a reporter for a local newspaper.

It should be noted that the organizational and instructional innovations at Dewey fit together to constitute a large-scale reform of traditional secondary education. The longer school day, for example, made it more feasible to pursue both basic academic and independent learning goals. Reorganization of classes during the school year not only provided greater assistance for low achievers but also allowed other students to schedule independent study and to enroll in academic electives supervised by faculty members selected for their willingness to work in this type of setting.

School-Within-a-School Unit in Kansas City, Mo.

The School-Within-a-School (SWAS) program at senior high schools in Kansas City was designed to help students low in reading achievement improve their comprehension and to otherwise motivate and prepare them to succeed in academic studies. Established at the ninth-grade level in all but one of Kansas City's senior high schools, the SWAS program typically assigns 80 to 100 students to receive academic instruction from four or five teachers of English/language arts, math, reading, social studies, and, in some cases, science. A teacher coordinator serves at least half-time. (Since Kansas City high schools are relatively small, SWAS enrolls a substantial proportion of the ninth-grade population.)

This organizational model can be utilized with some adaptation in any comprehensive high school that enrolls a significant number of students who cannot function well in regular classes without major intervention. As Keefe pointed out (1986), many ways exist to organize an effective school-within-a-school in the typical high school.

Placement in the Kansas City SWAS is based on academic achievement scores; teacher, counselor, and administrator judgment; attendance records; and other considerations, with particular attention given to functional comprehension scores on the Degrees of Reading Power Test.

Students who are virtually nonreaders or are severely disruptive generally are not assigned to SWAS because they require an even stronger intervention. Selection criteria are not conceived as homogeneous grouping or tracking, but rather as a form of leveling that identifies a band of students who can benefit from a year of intense special assistance and then participate in regular school programming.

Teachers appointed to SWAS are selected for their willingness and ability to work with at-risk students. Within the SWAS structure, students are taught in relatively small classes. Teachers are provided with training and other forms of assistance to implement the program goals.

Program features include the following:

- Content-area materials are below students' frustration level for independent work and slightly above their instructional level for classroom instruction.
- Instructional methods emphasize comprehension-development techniques such as those described by Harris and Cooper (1985).
- Teachers have common planning periods, intended in part to improve the coordination of instruction, and particularly to provide reinforcement across classes—a necessity for low achievers. Teacher teams agree on the selection and use of texts, student grading policies and practices, communication with parents, and other matters.
- Highly motivating experiences are offered to students. These include academic competition between teams and schools, college visits, conferences with local community leaders, and cultural events.
- Degrees of Reading Power scores and other data are collected regularly to assess student progress and to evaluate the instructional improvement efforts of the program.
- Intensive staff development is offered, including summer training, Saturday sessions, and seminars during the regular school day. Summer staff development time has been particularly valuable in providing teachers with the technical assistance to coordinate curriculum and instruction across subject areas and to share ideas and materials across schools.

When implemented effectively, the Kansas City SWAS program can be very successful. Among ninth-grade units at the high schools, for example, impressive gains have been registered in student attendance, performance on state basic-skills tests, and, in some places, reading comprehension.

Some Conclusions

Space limitations prohibit a full analysis of all the important considerations for administrators interested in restructuring secondary schools to improve student performance. The descriptions of restructured high schools cited above, however, suggest several issues that should be taken into account.

1. Commonalities among the schools and approaches point up several kinds of changes that may be prerequisite to radical restructuring. These include:

- Concentration on improving comprehension and other basic learning skills for low achievers. We use the term ''basic learning skills'' to distinguish them from other basic skills that focus on low-level processes such as language mechanics in reading and simple computation in math. To the extent that low achievers do not improve their comprehension and other information-processing skills, they will not be prepared for ''regular'' high school work, and schools with many low achievers will continue to flounder.
- Provision for alternative types of learning arrangements and experiences that allow students to pursue topics of special interest that will motivate them to improve their performance. These alternatives include mini-schools and schools-within-a-school, ''institutes'' involving blocks of courses, and opportunities to learn outside the four walls of the traditional school.
- Substantial staff turnover and/or selection, and staff development, resulting in the appointment of teachers who are willing and able to work effectively with students who have not succeeded in traditional settings.
- In inner-city schools enrolling mostly working-class or poverty-level students, very strong discipline policies consistently enforced by teachers who are personally committed to maintaining an orderly school and who implement these ''no-nonsense'' policies in large part through personal contact with students (not by bureaucratic application of endless rules and regulations).

2. Districts must provide small, alternative arrangements for students who are consistently disruptive but who are currently allowed to subvert improvement efforts or are expelled. Alternatives can include mini-schools, storefront schools, street academies, high-school outposts, and semi-detached schools-within-a-school (Levine, 1975; Wehlage, 1988). Without alternatives of this kind, most inner-city schools will continue to swing between expulsion patterns that some constituents view as excessive and improvement efforts that are undercut by disruptive students.

3. For previously low achievers to succeed in regular high school classes, some form of leveling usually will be needed to improve comprehension and other learning skills. In many working-class schools such as South Boston and the Kansas City ninth-grade SWAS units, leveling will take the form of separate grouping for poor readers and adequate and superior readers, for a year or two, for part or much of the school day. We use the term leveling here to contrast this intervention with homogeneous grouping and tracking approaches that establish many levels and place low achievers permanently or indefinitely in a series of remedial courses.

4. Among the most important characteristics of successfully restructured high schools are the insistence on higher levels of student performance and responsibility and the support necessary for students to meet their responsibilities. Insistence combined with support for higher performance are apparent, for example, in Washington High School's requirement that failing students receive additional instruction on Saturday; in South Boston's strict attendance policies and emphasis on personal guidance and development; and in John Dewey's independent learning opportunities requiring high standards of performance at numerous subject-area centers.

Insistence on high standards must be planned and adhered to even in the face of the difficulties that are sure to arise in implementation. The regular hall sweeps at Washington High School seem no different in kind from those at other inner-city schools. The real difference lies in their frequency and continuation over long periods of time.

5. Little or nothing in the school descriptions above conflicts with the effective school characteristics identified in other sources. The five characteristics (leadership, positive climate, high expectations, frequent monitoring of student progress, and emphasis on academic learning) described by Wilbur Brookover, Ron Edmonds, and their colleagues, are evident at the restructured schools.

Also present are the four characteristics (organizational arrangements for low achievers, emphasis on higher-order skills, institutionalization of high expectations, focus on students' personal growth and development) we found at unusually successful inner-city intermediate schools (Levine, Levine, and Eubanks, 1984).

Other elements are apparent in our descriptions (reduced tracking, and building-level control of variables such as staff selection and instructional organization) which Chubb and Moe (1986) found to characterize unusually effective high schools. Organizational restructuring of schools has also helped overcome the emphasis on mindless "coverage" of material that many observers see in traditional schools.

Indeed, restructured organizational arrangements and related changes in policy and practice probably are a prerequisite for achieving effectiveness at the senior high school level.

References

Chubb, J.E., and Moe, T.M. "No School Is an Island: Politics, Markets and Education." *The Brookings Review* 4(1986):21-28.

Harris, T.L., and Cooper, E.U., eds. *Reading, Thinking, and Concept Development*. New York: College Entrance Examination Board, 1985.

Keefe, J.W. ''How Do You Find the Time?'' In *Rethinking Reform: The Principal's Dilemma*, edited by H.J. Walberg and J.W. Keefe. Reston, Va.: National Association of Secondary School Principals, 1986.

Kozberg, G., and Winegar, J. ''The South Boston Story: Implications for Secondary Schools.'' *Phi Delta Kappan* 62(1981):565-567.

Levine, D.U. ''Educating Alienated Inner City Youth: Lessons from the Street Academies.'' *The Journal of Negro Education* 44(1975): 139-148.

Levine, D.U.; Levine, R.F.; and Eubanks, E.E. ''Characteristics of Effective Inner-City Intermediate Schools.'' *Phi Delta Kappan* 65 (1984):707-711.

Levine, S. ''The John Dewey High School Adventure.'' *Phi Delta Kappan* 53(1971):108-110.

Project on Adolescent Literacy. ''Curriculum and Instruction.'' *Common Focus* 8(1987):3.

Schain, R. L. ''Ninth Annual Report to the Parents.'' Brooklyn, N.Y.: George W. Wingate High School, 1980.

U.S. Department of Education. *Schools That Work Educating Disadvantaged Children*. Washington, D.C.: U.S. Government Printing Office, 1987.

Wehlage, G.G. ''Dropping Out: Can Schools Be Expected To Prevent It?'' Paper delivered at the annual meeting of the American Educational Research Association, New Orleans, April 1988.

CHAPTER 7

Paradigm High School

MARY ANNE RAYWID

PARADIGM HIGH SCHOOL has many of the features currently sought through restructuring: extensive personalization, a strong and distinctive ethos, an emphasis on the school as a community, and a continuing concern with the quality of work life within the school—all experienced by the students, who are expected to function as workers, and by the teachers.

These attributes are sustained by a school-within-a-school organization, increased school site autonomy, strengthened collaboration and collective responsibility among teachers, and expanded, more flexible roles for all those within the school. These organizational features—the structure, the culture, and the climate—have in turn yielded programs that truly engage students and render teachers far more effective than most.

Paradigm High perceives its primary responsibility to be helping adolescents achieve adulthood. This necessitates considerably broader aims than academic learning. It calls, first, for a developmental focus—a preoccupation with growth and change within individuals—and it obligates an interest in various dimensions of maturation, with each individual's character as well as with his or her intellect. Paradigm is an environment in which there are no anonymous youngsters.

Despite the broader concerns, formal learning does not take a back seat at Paradigm High. The development of intellectual power is an aim in all academic study, and maximal intellectual power is the ultimate criterion for what a student pursues, rather than a standard list of courses to be taken or tests to be passed.

This focus calls for program differentiation. It also demands systematic efforts to ensure that intellectual power is reflected not only in the particular learnings and understandings pursued, but also in the identity each individual is forging, in the kind of autonomy, responsibility, and human connections each is fashioning. In short, character, as well as intellect, is the concern; development, as well as the achievement of academic skills and cultural literacy.

Paradigm's teachers take cultural literacy seriously, however, and discussions about common learnings are a continuing phenomenon. Instructional decisions seek to balance the need for commonality with concern for responsiveness to particular groups of youngsters. The compromise is often, but not always, agreement at the level of concepts, with the means to convey them left open.

Paradigm staff members recognize that a good school must stand for something; it must have a mission. Thus, Paradigm teachers have not been reluctant to discuss desired traits and to enunciate a character ideal. But they are also aware that differences in themselves, reflected in the surrounding community, make a single character ideal impossible.

Rather than abandon or so compromise a model that it becomes meaningless to all, the staff have divided Paradigm into four schools-within-a-school. Each has it own personnel and students, and each pursues a distinctive vision of schooling. A number of commonalities exist among the four, of course, and some major differences.

There are approximately 250 students and 10 teachers in each of Paradigm's four schools-within-the-school. They are known as the Challenge Team, the Social Services Academy, Sequoia Institute, and Media. Teachers evolved the four themes out of their own interests and those of students. Both teachers and students choose the particular school-within-a-school with which they are affiliated. The four options are carefully investigated by students. The choice represents the culminating project of an eighth-grade social studies unit on decision making. Most youngsters remain with their chosen school-within-a-school until graduation. Those who make a wrong choice, or whose interests change, are able to shift from one program to another.

Each school-within-a-school enjoys a degree of physical separation from the rest. Paradigm is built to look like a giant "X." Each of the four line segments represents a separate school-within-a-school. At the intersection of the four are the common areas they all share: the library, the gym, the auditorium. The full student body occasionally assembles for special activities, but customarily the four schools-within-the-school operate as separate units.

The commonalities are ensured in several ways. Both the district and the state in which Paradigm High School is located support the principle of "strategic independence" for innovative schools.[1] They acknowledge that school improvement cannot be accomplished through detailed external control, and have framed their expectations accordingly. General curricular goals have been set for Paradigm, but each of its four programs retains considerable leeway in determining the particular content and activities to best serve its students. This autonomy means that each of these schools-within-a-school has an "innovative charter."[2] It combines the opportunity to design the best program for a particular group with the responsibility for doing so.

---

1. As suggested by Chester E. Finn, Jr. in "Toward Strategic Independence: Nine Commandments for Enhancing School Effectiveness," *Phi Delta Kappan*, April 1984, pp. 518-524.
2. Mary Haywood Metz, "In Education, Magnets Attract Controversy," *NEA Today*, January 1988, pp. 54-60.

Teachers meet this responsibility through continuing contact and collaboration. Every Wednesday morning, all Paradigm students participate in service learning activities outside the school, and staff members of each of the four subschools meet. The typical pattern involves two meetings each Wednesday morning. The 10 teachers of each school-within-a-school usually get together for an early breakfast to discuss matters of general concern. Then smaller groups who are team teaching, or who share other specific responsibilities, meet to work on curriculum or special assignments.

The four schools within Paradigm High are constituted along somewhat different lines because the interests and needs of those involved divide this way. For some, the prospect of particular experiences and activities draw them to the Challenge Team. Others already attracted to the human and social services attend the Social Services Academy. But its particular orientation also makes the Academy attractive to youngsters who do not yet have a sociocentric orientation (to be described in a few minutes).

Sequoia Institute is frequently the choice of those who might have been served by a traditional high school. They are academically motivated, receptive to exploring the several disciplines, and learn well from conventional methods. The fourth program is known simply as ''Media,'' but more formally as The School of Communications Arts. It attracts youngsters who want to write, draw, or perform.

Each of the four subschools has its own distinctive organization and culture, as well as unique curricular emphasis. Staff members recognize that Paradigm's curricular specializations favor the humanities and social sciences, but the programs accord with the students' preferences. Each of the four provides a full curriculum, and students with strong interests in science or math apparently satisfy them within the Sequoia program.

Whether new programs should be added is one of the concerns of Paradigm's principal. She helped in planning the four existing schools-within-the-school and is their staunch champion. District guidelines for innovative programs call for extensive teacher involvement in their design and direction, and the particular arrangements for Paradigm were designed at the school.

The major criterion was keeping decisions as close to the classroom as possible. A teacher director for each program is elected by its staff members for a four-year term. All four teacher-directors run a student advisory group and teach one class. Beyond that, their functions pertain more to leadership than management. The goal and value agreement and the small size of each unit reduce the need for oversight. Fewer rules are necessary and fewer steps are required to make sure they are carried out. Daily operation is shifted from formal to informal structures, and the administrative contribution most needed is that of sustaining relationships and traditions.

The role of Paradigm's principal is analogous to that of a supervising principal or district official. She coordinates among the four programs, represents them to the district, and provides interactions with feeder and other schools as well as with the community. Community relations occupy a substantial amount of her time, because Paradigm depends on a number of other agencies and organizations to support its programs and the social services some students require.

The four schools-within-a-school differ in a number of their arrangements and policies, but there are some commonalities. First of all, students are not limited to the program in which they are enrolled. Many take all their work in their subschools, but several other opportunities remain open to them. They may occasionally register for a particular course in one of the other programs. Some also take one or two courses at a local college or university. One of the programs may arrange an ancillary course by someone in the community. A network cameraman, for instance, recently taught a course in television camerawork at his studio for Media students, and a professor of medicine taught a course in human anatomy at a local university for Sequoia students.

Each of the four programs offers students the opportunity to do independent study under the supervision of a knowledgeable individual. This option enables some students to do advanced work in a particular field and others to pursue different sorts of interests. Some of the independent study arrangements are internships; some primarily involve library research; some are design and construction projects. The supervisors—called mentors—include Paradigm teachers as well as local business or professional people. All Paradigm students take one independent study course; many take several.

A third common feature of all Paradigm High School programs is service learning. Each youngster is involved each year in substantial volunteer activity (averaging from three to six hours a week) that is carefully integrated with classroom work, although the four programs handle the integration somewhat differently. Thus, for the Challenge Team, service learning is an integral part of civic education and of a major global awareness project for each student. For Social Services Academy students, volunteer activities are the application and testing ground for much that they are learning about human beings, roles, and organizational operation. For many, it functions as career exploration as well. But for all Paradigm students, service learning is an opportunity to make a genuine contribution to the lives of other human beings.

A fourth common feature is a strong emphasis on the school-within-a-school as a distinctive community. Considerable self-consciousness exists about the particular kind of community each is, and students quickly become aware of the traditions and ideals associated with the program they have chosen. All Paradigm students pursue some formal study of education, but they do so in different ways and with different emphases.

In all four programs, there is examination of school as an institution and as a socio-cultural system, and of differing visions of what it is to be educated. Two things come out of this for most Paradigm students: One is an unusual sophistication about the nature of education and what they are doing in school. The second is a strong sense of affiliation with and loyalty to the program they have selected.

Yet another commonality among all four schools-within-the-school is the student advisory group.[3] Here again, differences are present in the way the groups operate, but in each subschool they perform important functions. Each teacher has an advisory group, and in most cases becomes the person who knows each group member better than does any other adult in the school. At various time, advisers serve as ombudsmen and advocates, as well as mentors and confidantes for their advisees.

Paradigm staff members are aware that not every human being can respond to every other. They believe that every youngster in the school should have at least one adult with whom he or she can connect. They agree that maximizing individual development seriously obligates detailed acquaintance with each youngster's progress. Since advisory groups in all programs meet regularly, and the students remain as a group until graduation, all members come to know each other well. For many of them, the group becomes the primary point of identification within the school.

One more structural feature is found in one form or another in all four of Paradigm's schools-within-a-school. It is called "The Committee on Discombobulation," or "The Boatrockers," or "The Regenerators." The Social Services Academy calls it "The Committee for Examining Cultural Assumptions and Adapting to the Changing Scene." The function is self-scrutiny.

Each of the groups is charged with looking at the program to unearth and examine the otherwise assumed and taken-for-granted, or what seems to be missing or what is not working. On occasion, the groups function in an ombudsman role. More typically, they test the continuing validity of their program's presuppositions. This is Paradigm's way of maintaining each of the four schools-within-a-school as a self-renewing system, and to prevent the strong points of each from blinding personnel to the need for possible changes.

Social Services Academy

The Social Services Academy is carefully designed to avoid tracking students on the basis of their ability. Its focus on applied social science attracts youngsters who are prospective social workers, psychologists,

---

3. See J. Lloyd Trump, *A School for Everyone* (Reston, Va.: NASSP, 1977); and James W. Keefe, "Advisement—A Helping Role," *The Practitioner*, NASSP, June 1983.

lawyers, and teachers. On the other hand, Academy activities have particular appeal for youngsters who have not been much interested in school. The action orientation initially attracts them, but many eventually find the content compelling.

Academy courses include a popular offering in cultural journalism. Students interview community residents on a different socially significant theme each semester, and then issue a publication containing their carefully-honed essays. The Academy also runs a Consumer Action Service that takes the cases of people wronged by local merchants, and of citizens who claim unjust treatment by municipal institutions. The student advocates get valuable lessons in consumer protection and civic action. The service has earned the respect and appreciation of local residents. There is a course in street law that holds a strong attraction for some youngsters. They emerge with a good understanding of the guarantees of the Bill of Rights, as well as with some knowledge of civil and criminal law.

The Academy emphasizes collaborative learning through group assignments. Cooperative learning strategies lead to tutorial programs in which some Academy students serve as peer tutors to others, and prepare them to tutor younger students. There is also a unique language program in which Hispanic students instruct their Anglo classmates in Spanish and receive coaching in English in return. Academy students are sought as teacher aides in local elementary schools, and have tutored and assisted handicapped college students.

The School of Communication Arts (“Media”)

Media is a popular program that draws some of its students by its content and others by its activities. Media publishes the school newspaper and a literary magazine. Its students run a weekly program at a local radio station which began as a typical teen show but has evolved into commentary on contemporary events and conditions. Other Media students assist at the local public television station, and a few have been fortunate enough to have interned there.

Media offers choices and specialization opportunities, and the chance to take on adult challenges. It is also a place where teachers strive continually to blend the theoretical and the practical. Thus, English instruction emphasizes writing for publication, and polished articles are, indeed, published. Literature, science, and social studies courses all feature the kind of analysis that helps youngsters to critique their own work, and to have something to say.

One of the major features of Media is its close ties to the community. It draws a large advisory board of professionals and managers from the communications industry. Its members address classes, and some serve as mentors. Advisory board ideas and advice have been appreciated as much as the equipment some have donated to Media. Another form of support most advisory board members have offered is summer employment for Media students.

About 70 percent of Media graduates go on to college, many more than those planning to do so on entrance. Most of these youngsters, and the graduates who enter the work force right away, pursue careers related to the communications industry.

Sequoia Institute

Sequoia is the most traditional of Paradigm's four schools-within-a-school, but it is not simply a small conventional high school. Sequoia students tend to have an interest in intellectual matters. Staff members nurture this interest carefully, and place a premium on learner engagement with content. One means of engagement is the presentation of traditional fare in novel contexts.

A course on "Albert Einstein and the 20th Century," for example, combines advanced physics, literature, and introductory philosophy. A course in "The Civil War and Reconstruction: Black Perspectives" teaches historiography as well as literature and history. "The Mathematicians Who Built the Pyramids" combines advanced mathematics and a fascinating look at ancient history. "Ocean Ecology" combines chemistry, currents, and marine biology.

Sequoia staff take seriously the "less is more" axiom. Students take fewer classes for longer periods each day, and are pressed to think more penetratingly.[4] Teachers recognize that different kinds of teaching are essential to different types of knowledge goals (transmitting organized knowledge, developing intellectual skills, and cultivating understanding), and they seek to ensure a balance among didactic, coaching, and Socratic approaches.[5]

Sequoia students display less need for experiential learning than students in Paradigm's other three programs, and they take particular pride in academic accomplishment. Their debate team is a consistent winner, as are their "mathletes."

The Challenge Team

The Challenge Team is Paradigm's least orthodox program. Student progress is measured by demonstrating competence through a combination of classwork, travel, and independent activity both inside and outside the school.

4. As urged by Theodore Sizer in *Horace's Compromise: The Dilemma of the American High School* (Boston: Houghton Mifflin, 1984).

5. See Mortimer J. Adler, *The Paidea Proposal: An Educational Manifesto* (New York: Macmillan, 1982).

Students choose the Team for a variety of reasons. Many are attracted by the extent to which programs are individualized. Some appear to have been academically stifled in other schools. For almost all, the Team is an initial cultural shock as they acclimate to the transfer of responsibility from teacher to student. Challenge Team classes represent resources and opportunities, as do teachers, libraries and agencies, community members, trips, and other kinds of experiences.

The Challenge program requires competence in 49 academic, personal, consumer, civic, and career skills. Classes and activities present opportunities for acquiring and demonstrating competencies. When students have acquired them, they are eligible to propose extended "Passage" projects combining these skills. Passages of six different types must be completed—experiences involving adventure, career exploration, creativity, global awareness, logical inquiry, and practical skills.

The global awareness Passage, for example, involves a two or three-year sequence of carefully coordinated activity. Each youngster must select a world problem, study its occurrence at national and local levels, and then attempt to do something about it locally. Thus, a student might select world hunger as a Global Awareness problem, pursue it in classes and assignment options, undertake independent study to learn how the problem is handled in this country and in at least one other country, and then do volunteer work at a local soup kitchen or in an agency that aids the homeless.

The Challenge Team is a demanding, innovative program that responds well to the needs of young people who are impatient with the more passive role of the traditional student.

Paradigm Perspectives

These four distinctive programs at Paradigm High are possible because the school is located in a state that exempts schools from curricular and other mandates for purposes of innovation. Its program is sufficiently successful that it is being continued as a state education department approved demonstration project.

It has not been saddled with the batteries of standardized tests that have blocked reform in other schools. Nevertheless, its district does expect to see evidence of accomplishment across a broad spectrum. As part of its "innovative charter," each school-within-a-school is invited to assemble its own portfolio of evidence for annual public discussion with the board of education.

All four programs currently use a combination of normed tests and documentation of their achievements. Because the four sets of evidence are not identical, comparisons among the four programs are not easily drawn. Many Paradigm constituents view this as a distinct advantage, particularly since all the portfolios contain sufficient material about progress and accomplishment.

Some important assumptions are shared by all Paradigm programs. First, all see the teacher as the school's primary educational resource and the critical element in school improvement. Second, teacher-student relationships are considered of central importance, and this value is applied to both student and teacher assignments, load, and scheduling. Third, all four programs have expanded the roles of teachers and students as the school's central players. Both students and teachers have broader responsibilities than in the comprehensive high school.

Fourth, none of the programs takes student motivation for granted; all believe it can be cultivated. Through content, organization, presentation, and activities, all four programs seek to maintain student engagement. Finally, each program has a deliberate strategy for building student self-esteem and a sense of efficacy. This is considered to be of instrumental importance to student accomplishment.

Paradigm High is fictional and it is not without its problems—but they are problems refreshingly different from those with which we are familiar. Both the formal procedures and the informal traditions described here make the problems available to collective examination and solution. Some may find Paradigm's schools-within-a-school fanciful, but it seems worth noting that few of the features described are fictional. Almost all are in operation in at least one school or program known to the author.

The features have been assembled from a lengthy list of schools that includes: Metro High School, Chicago; Jefferson County Open High School, Evergreen, Colo.; Syosset High School, Syosset, N.Y.; Shoreham-Wading River Middle School, Shoreham, N.Y.; Media Academy, Oakland, Calif.; Village School, Great Neck, N.Y.; Central Park East Secondary School and Community School District 4, N.Y.; Metropolitan Learning Center, Portland, Oreg.; St. Paul Open School, St. Paul, Minn.; Metro High School, St. Louis, Mo.; and Central High School, Dubuque, Iowa.

CHAPTER 8

A Restructured School

JOE NATHAN

- A teacher was ready to quit education after 10 years. Most of her students and parents felt she was an excellent teacher. One of the principals with whom she worked had ranked her as outstanding, but other administrators did not like her creative approaches, including numerous field trips, nontraditional seating assignments, and frequent requests from parents that students be placed in her courses. One summer she decided to try teaching in a newly established alternative program in the district. If this didn't work, she would quit. She is still teaching 15 years later, and is recognized as extraordinary. She says this school kept her in education.
- A 17-year-old youth was expelled from his previous high schoool after striking a teacher who had ordered him to remove his hat, and then knocked the hat off his head when he would not follow directions. At his new school, the youngster became involved in a Consumer Action class which studied and solved adult problems referred by community members. Gradually, his behavior and academic skills improved. After his name appeared in a newspaper article about the class, the student told his instructor that "I often thought I might have my name in the newspaper . . . and I even thought I might have my picture in the newspaper. But I never thought it would be for something good."
- On the first day of school, a 13-year-old student was asked to read to a frightened 5-year-old. They became good friends. Several months later, the 13-year-old explained her dramatic improvement: "When you asked me to help Beth, that changed the way I thought about myself. It was the first time anyone in a school made me feel like I was worth something."

These stories come from the St. Paul Open School, an alternative program run by the St. Paul, Minn., Public Schools. More than 50,000 people from around the world have visited the Open School during its first decade as a restructured school.

The St. Paul Open School welcomed its first 500 students, ages 5-18, in September 1971. The St. Paul Public Schools started the program after several thousand parents and educators attended meetings, developed plans, raised federal and foundation funds, and asked to participate. During its first month, the school was featured on the "Today Show."

Within five years, it received a Pacesetter Award from the U.S. Department of Education, representing selection as a "carefully evaluated, proven innovation worthy of national replication."[1] The award brought federal grants, allowing Open School staff members to work with other educators who wanted to replicate parts of the program.

The parents and educators who established this school wanted it to reflect the most advanced thinking about how children learn. This meant that they had to seek exemptions from many state regulations about how schools are organized and operated. The school's founders agreed on the following basic principles:

1. Each student should have an individual program of courses and other learning opportunities, developed cooperatively by parents, students, and staff members.
2. Each teacher and administrator should spend some time teaching and some time advising a group of students.
3. Parents, teachers, and students should have the opportunity to help make decisions about school policies and procedures.
4. The school should function as a headquarters for learning, with many important activities taking place outside the school.
5. Students should have the opportunity to learn with and from a variety of people.
6. New procedures should be developed for graduation.
7. Students should be involved in classes and other activities based on interest and ability, not age. The school would enroll students from 5 to 18 years of age.
8. The school should have considerable autonomy to determine how its budget is spent. After a two or three year startup period during which the school is equipped, the school would receive the same per pupil allotment as other district schools.
9. The school would seek a faculty and student body that reflected the racial diversity of the city and that had voluntarily chosen the school.
10. Developing higher order problem solving and thinking skills should involve helping solve real problems, and make a difference in other peoples' lives.

After some discussion, the Minnesota Board of Education agreed to waive most of its requirements as long as the Open School agreed to measure students' progress, accept responsibility for results, and share them with the public. (This arrangement is similar to that proposed in the 1986 National Governors' Association report, *Time for Results*, in which governors offered "to give up a lot of state regulatory control—even to

---

1. Much more information about the Open School's successes and problems is available in Joe Nathan, *Free To Teach: Achieving Equity and Excellence in Schools* (Minneapolis, Minn.: Harper-Row/Winston, 1984).

fight for changes in the law to make that happen—if schools and school districts would be accountable for the results.''

The Open School accepted the challenge. The first change approved by the Minnesota State Board of Education involved ages of students. Open School parents and educators wanted the school to operate something like a successful family or one-room school. That meant students, ages 5 through 18, moving at their own pace. Students of different ages attend class together, based on their skill level and interest, rather than their age. Open School 12 to 15-year-olds tend to be much calmer than in other schools because they have older role models. The older students constantly help the younger ones.

This assistance is critical: All Open School students are expected to help the school. In fact, it is a graduation requirement. School service may include tutoring, cleanup patrol, making signs, working as an office or teacher assistant, or working on a committee.

Many classes include some form of community service—helping solve consumer problems, assisting with political campaigns, helping design and build a playground, etc.

Another change approved by the state department of education involved graduation requirements. Like most other states, Minnesota requires that students accumulate credits for graduation in certain subjects (such as English, social studies, mathematics, and science). In order to earn credits, students must spend a certain amount of time in these courses.

This system dates to the early 1900s when the Carnegie Endowment for the Advancement of Teaching suggested it to distinguish between high schools and colleges. Carnegie wanted to improve the status of college professors and to award funds for their pensions. Since there were few clear distinctions in 1910 between high schools and colleges, Carnegie decided that institutions eligible for its grants would have to establish graduation requirements based on accumulation of 14 ''standard'' (soon known as ''Carnegie'') units, earned by attending classes for 120 60-minute periods.[2] This system is convenient, but it does not correspond with what we know about how young people learn.

With state approval, the Open School established that, for graduation, students must demonstrate certain basic and applied skills and knowledge. The Open School graduation committee liked the way states awarded drivers' licenses. Applicants had to pass both paper and pencil and ''real world performance'' examinations. After surveying employers and postsecondary institutions, the school selected six areas in which

---

2. Joe Nathan and Wayne Jennings, ''Educational Bait-and-Switch,'' *Phi Delta Kappan*, May 1978, pp. 621-615; or Joe Nathan, ''Graduation Requirements: Illusions and Realities.'' Master's thesis, University of Minnesota, June 1974.

prospective graduates would have to demonstrate knowledge: career awareness, consumer awareness, information finding, community knowledge and service, personal and interpersonal skills and communication, and cultural awareness.

Each student developed a packet of validations, with teachers, employers, parents, and others documenting that the student had demonstrated the required skill. This system replaced grades and credits. For 17 years, colleges and universities have accepted this system. Several Open School students have received National Merit Scholar designation, and a number have attended prestigious colleges and universities.

The graduation system provided a framework for parents and students to meet with advisers to plan individual programs. Older students exercised more influence on their schedules than younger students, but every student helped to determine his or her activities based on skills, interests, and priorities. Classes, learning labs, field trips, internships, individual projects, and employment are among the options that faculty members arrange and supervise. Each student has a written plan that is evaluated periodically during the year. Parents, students, and advisers meet three to four times each year to discuss progress and to plan for the future.

The entire North American continent is considered the school's learning environment, so its students and parents have a much wider range of options than the traditional course schedule. Classes often include field trips to geographic and historic sites throughout the state, and sometimes the nation. Geology classes go to the Grand Canyon; Spanish classes have a yearly exchange with a school in Mexico; a Civil War class travels to Gettysburg; and an urban studies class goes to 10 eastern cities.

Teenage students also have internships in local businesses and social service agencies.

The role of staff members is quite different than in most traditional schools. Teachers function as advisers for 25 to 30 students, in addition to teaching courses. Moreover, teachers serve on all committees, including those that determine how to spend the budget and evaluate school and individual performance, as well as on the advisory council that works with the principal to set school policy. Long before the current talk about teacher professionalism, St. Paul Open School staff members had extraordinary opportunities to decide how their programs would function.

The Open School began its seventeenth year in September 1988. Unlike many other innovations, it has survived changes in building and district leadership, new national educational reform trends, and movement from its original home to a second and then a third building. Despite many difficulties, the school's original principles remain, and hundreds of students have benefited.

The school's experiences may assist advocates of restructured schooling. Here are several lessons learned at St. Paul Open School.

1. *We must change our primary view of youth from recipients of service to thoughtful, creative providers of service to others.*

Central to acquiring skills and becoming an active citizen in a democracy is learning how one person can make a positive difference. Youngsters need to know that they are worthwhile—a realization that often produces remarkable improvements in attitude and achievement. Young people have a lot to learn from teachers and parents, but in the process of growing, they can and should learn to share and serve.[3]

2. *Very few schools are appropriate for all students, parents, or teachers.*

The Open School succeeded with hundreds of students who had not been particularly successful in other places. Some bright students who had made acceptable progress in traditional schools became outstanding students at the Open School. Other students viewed as retarded blossomed at the Open School.

Some missed receiving grades. Others wished for a larger school with a more formal social environment.

A distinctive school will attract some excellent teachers while it repels other outstanding teachers. Some of St. Paul Public School's finest teachers work at the Open School. Others have tried it and say they prefer the conventional school.

The Open School is not a good place for everyone. This view is consistent with steadily accumulating research showing that people have very different learning styles, and that is impossible to develop "one best system."

3. *Departing dramatically from conventional practice will allow some students to achieve much higher levels of achievement than previously thought possible.*

Some of the Open School's most successful students failed miserably in traditional schools. They are among the school's strongest, most persuasive advocates.

4. *Shared decision making requires constant attention and learning for all who are involved.*

Most parents, teachers, and administrators are not trained to work together. Many colleges do not teach prospective educators how to hold

3. The most recent, eloquent statement on this subject is by Eliot Wigginton, *Sometimes a Shining Moment* (New York: Anchor Press, 1985).

parent conferences or how to run effective committee meetings. Collective decision making is often tiresome, slow, and even painful. But most people at the Open School are glad they have the opportunity to make decisions. Building commitment to the program, in part by sharing decisions about it, is an important reason the school has survived for 16 years.

5. *Educators must continue to critique and revise their programs based on evaluative measures, including student achievement and surveys of graduates.*

Many of the most helpful suggestions for improvement come from graduates. The Open School has benefited because it listened carefully to former students and parents, and because it was able to document significant student growth and achievement.

6. *Educators planning to depart dramatically from conventional patterns should be prepared for constant battles with other educators.*

Unfortunately, some educators think there is "one best system" for operating a school. They resist and criticize innovations, often on the basis of hearsay rather than actual observation. More important, school districts and state systems (budget, licensing, reporting, etc.) are based on the conventional way of doing things. Continuing pressure exists to move toward the norm.

7. *Educators working for fundamental change in the way schools are organized and operate will have to look hard to find supportive higher education institutions.*

Many teacher education departments refused to place student teachers at the Open School. Many education professors turned down offers from Open School staff members to speak to their classes, or to bring university classes to the school, even after it won national awards.

8. *Well-designed and implemented innovations benefit from, but can survive the loss of, outstanding leadership.*

The Open School's marvelous first principal, Wayne Jennings, worked with parents and staff to build community support for the school. When Jennings left after nine years, the school missed his vision and knowledge. But it survived and continues to develop because of an outstanding staff, deeply committed parents, and common-sense learning strategies.

The Open School has had its best years, however, when the principal shares the school's philosophy and uses his or her talents and energy to promote or improve practices consistent with that philosophy. Teachers, parents, and students have suffered when administrators disagreed with or were apathetic to the school's principles. Leadership makes an enormous difference.

Former *New York Times* education editor Fred Hechinger is one of this nation's most thoughtful and informed reform advocates. Recently, Hechinger (1987) wrote about educators' attitudes toward success:

> Unfortunately, educators often pay no attention to success stories in newspapers or on television unless they are about their own schools. And when they do pay attention, they often complain that the reporter has been hoodwinked by a teacher or a principal seeking publicity. Or they cite particular circumstances that make it impossible for them to do the same thing . . . (education reform) remains a dim hope as long as many educators, deliberately or not, fail to visit those islands of excellence and try to learn from them. Since the Deborah Meiers (recently honored for her work at alternative public schools in New York City) cannot be cloned, they might at least be studied.

The St. Paul Open School began and continues because a few brave people—educators, parents, and students—committed themselves. They believed traditional schools were not healthy places for some educators and some youngsters. They read, listened, thought, argued, and learned how to make schooling and learning better. This chapter will have served its purpose if others are encouraged to do the same.

References

Hechinger, Fred. "The Short Life of the Success Story." *The New York Times*, July 7, 1987, p. 16.

National Governors' Association. *Time for Results: The Governors' 1991 Report on Education*. Washington, D.C.:NGA, 1986, p.4.

CHAPTER 9
An Information Age School

ROBERT ST. CLAIR

DISCUSSION OF THE "Information Age" inevitably causes the spotlight to be focused on schools. Schools are the foundation upon which an information society is built.

Against this background, educators have been characterized as holding their own against difficult odds by the charitable, and as saboteurs by the critical. It is probably fair to say that, to date, technology and the changes it has produced in American culture have done more to education than for it.

The purpose of this chapter is to encourage school leaders to see technology as an ally and to adopt a positive attitude toward it. Included are specific illustrations of ways technology can be applied to solve some of the perplexing problems facing the schools.

Adapting the tools of technology to the field of education will not be an easy task. It will require time, resources, and creativity. Schools are awash in information and excessive demands are made on those who work in them. Moreover, many educators lack training in the applications and forms of assistance that technology offers.

What are the ways that technology can help deal with the problems confronting our schools? It is not possible to cite schools that have incorporated all the workable strategies, but several alternatives listed below are based on technology that is already here.

First, we need to provide those who work in schools with time to learn as well as time to teach or supervise. A monumental problem for our schools is that the tasks of planning, curriculum, and instruction are viewed as relatively static. This underlying assumption about our delivery system was defensible until knowledge and information began to accumulate at a totally unprecedented rate. Thoughtful people, assisted by machines, are responsible for that knowledge explosion. It will take thoughtful school people, assisted by machines, to accommodate the change in our schools.

Time is in short supply, but dollars are also scarce. How can schools afford the extra time for teachers and administrators to learn and to develop new programs while they carry out current responsibilities? At present, we acquire time by extending the work day, by sending the students home, or by bringing in substitutes for part of the staff. None of these practices is without substantial cost in money or human resources, and none provides adequate time. Training school staff members to be technologically literate cannot be accommodated under such a system.

The good news is that many of the skills required by the newest hardware can be taught by the machines themselves. Today's "smart" machines not only occasion change, but can teach its applications. Computer technology, for example, now makes it possible to generate multiple versions of a school master schedule for a given year. Seven 55-minute periods can become six 64-minute periods, and one-seventh of the faculty can be relieved of potential teaching assignments.

This strategy provides time for extensive inservice, planning, or curriculum development without the cost of substitutes or subtracting substantially from the quality of instruction. In this schedule, teachers have longer blocks of time for learning and planning as well as for teaching and evaluating. Scheduling is still a time-consuming and labor intensive task, but software development has reached the stage where multiple schedules are readily feasible.

Faculty members need to experience the benefits as well as the burdens of technology. What if technology were applied to the challenge of direct, day-to-day evaluation of student achievement? Could the enormous burdens of grade reporting and recording be made easier for the teacher and the results more accessible for students and parents?

Not only does such technology exist, but bits and pieces of the computer software are already on the market. With the appropriate computer and software support, teachers can enter evaluations of their students into an electronic grade book. The system can record scores by keystroke or by an optical scanner and can be linked to the school's formal grade reporting system to obviate reentry of data at the end of the marking period. The system can generate reports more frequently for those youngsters having a difficult time keeping up with assignments. It is well documented that ongoing and immediate feedback is a boost to learning. The system makes it possible for all students to have an up-to-date report on their learning status at any time during the year.

Working with such a system can provide direct benefits to the teacher and spark other applications of technology to support learning. The teacher uses the technology as a tool. It is not the presence of technology that raises complaints about dehumanization. It is the impersonal and mechanical way in which that technology is sometimes applied to, or externally imposed upon, the lives of teachers and students that creates the problem. Sensitive school leaders must ensure that technology does things for people instead of to them.

A major cost in implementing a system based on technology is the amount of time needed to gain even a small degree of literacy. No one will bear that burden of technology more than the principal or assistant principal. Nevertheless, it is vitally important for administrators to be personally literate in the use of the various machines.

Ideally, administrators would purchase the machines and/or software for personal use. A school setting seldom provides the amount of uninterrupted time necessary to gain a beginner's proficiency with a given piece of hardware.

The best starting place is a basic word processor (WP) on a personal computer (PC). The ultimate payoff for such activity is that principals begin to develop an expanding knowledge base that, in turn, brings respect and credibility from faculty, students, and parents.

The public feels that people at the school know what they are doing. Information no longer is used primarily for reporting about the school, but for the leadership and management of the school. Feedback does not come in a huge dose at the end of the school year. It becomes a part of the daily routine. Decisions are based more frequently upon knowledge and less frequently upon intuition.

The amount of time required to gain a seemingly low level of proficiency on a computer or a specific piece of software may seem excessive, but the return on that investment comes quickly. A staffing report that required 8 to 10 hours of time can be completed in a matter of seconds—and with greater accuracy. Routine administrative memos can be updated and reproduced with minimal effort by administrators or secretaries. Budget development and supervision can be handled with accuracy and dispatch. Disciplinary data can be recorded in a way that makes month-to-month, year-to-year, or even period-to-period comparisons effortless. Rather than report impressions at faculty meetings, administrators can report fully substantiated facts.

The best news of all is that the cost of computers, information storage, and efficient printers has dropped to a level within the means of the vast majority of schools. "Stand alone" systems are now available to schools at a fraction of the cost of the mainframes required to deliver comparable services even a decade ago. Once such a system is installed in a given school, benefits begin to accrue at a surprising rate provided the building administrators are a part of the user network.

The bad news is that fully integrated systems are not very user friendly or responsive to the unique elements of a given school. Various hardware and software configurations are generally patched together. As administrators become better informed about the potential and the limitations of the computer, these applications will improve. Grade reporting is a good case in point. Separate packages are available, but the data generally are not integrated with other applications so that information can be moved easily from one application to another.

School people need to think about transmitting information electronically—a mind set that facilitates accuracy and effectiveness. Think, for example, about standardized test scores. Testing companies have such information available in electronic form, but usually convert it to gummed labels. School secretaries then affix the labels to student folders. It would be much easier to store and access the records electronically. Once the scores are incorporated in a student data base, accessible to the computer, they can be used for policy or curriculum decisions. They can be matched with profiles of student learning styles or assessment of levels of formal reasoning. The data can be used to assist in decisions about student scheduling or performance.

How many students, for example, with good abstract reasoning capacity and high standardized test scores in math and science are getting average or below-average grades in these subjects? Or, to go beyond the percentages involved and to support the human dimensions of the issue, who are those students and what strategies can help them realize their potential? Once again, the key is machines working *for* people. Keep in mind the importance of networking information within an entire school system. When possible, transmit electronically.

Fully integrated packages are especially important when using the information system for management. A comprehensive software package will help the system work for the administrator. If it is easy to load data from students' records into a research routine, then research will be facilitated. If research results can be easily transformed into graphic presentations, then these presentations will be developed. If all applications can be easily transferred to a publishing routine, then clear communication about results will be facilitated.

Too frequently, school people think in terms of discrete tasks. As a result, many vendors have prepared a series of small packages rather than integrated systems. It is critical to be able to move easily from one routine to another. In dealing with vendors, administrators should ask them to demonstrate the integration capabilities of their hardware/software configurations.

An efficient and effective information management system is vitally important to a school wishing to improve student learning. Think of the enormous potential for practical, school-based research. A carefully planned data base drawn from student records can allow teachers to examine the results of local reform efforts directly. Drawing data with specificity is a hallmark of the information society. Proposed improvements can be adopted, not on the basis of inference or faith, but on positive results gathered from field testing materials and methods with students and teachers at the local level.

Many school leaders have a difficult time understanding the magnitude of the changes which have already taken place outside schools. Many teachers and principals are like those persons in the early part of this century who were skeptical about the automobile; they liked their horses.

Given the conditions of the early roads and the performance of early autos, horses had some real advantages. It took a long time to develop dependable machines, a system of highways, and a utilitarian attitude about the automobile.

School people should approach technology with an open mind. How should educators organize for effective learning and instruction? What machines can help them get there? In order to answer the second part of that question, educators, especially school leaders, must invest the time to learn the functions of various machines and programs. Too frequently, teachers and administrators reject technology without first informing themselves.

Given time and encouragement, teachers begin to apply technology in their own disciplines. Simpler machines with more direct applications—such as overhead projectors and VCRs—have made their way quite easily into the classroom. Hand held calculators, once interdicted, are now commonly used in schools.

Videotape can also be used as a medium of instruction or expression. Education is very much rooted in print. The information age and its youngsters are not. Students can produce some remarkable video material, but their efforts are frequently relegated to second class status. The communication of information and ideas must be conceptualized in a broader sense if students are to be properly prepared for life in the next century.

One of the limiting factors educators currently face is the technology used in testing. Ironically, testing in traditionally defined and narrowly conceived subject matter areas is gaining in emphasis at the very time when new ways of looking at content and learning are available. Emphasis on testing and increased standards, both based on a traditional curriculum, assume that schools have already applied the lessons of the information age. There is little evidence that such a transformation has taken place.

Many once-sacred institutions have been swept away during the past two decades because they were unable to accommodate change. The attacks upon education during this same period of time have been relentless.

Educators can depend upon politicians and the public to let them know when something is wrong. Both are less dependable in providing workable solutions to educational problems.

Returning to the way things were will not suffice. Schools will be part of the future, and must find ways to accommodate it. Major responsibility for changes will fall upon principals and their assistants. These leaders must be informed about technology and support the needs and efforts of their teachers, students, and parents to prepare schools for the 21st century.

References

Dembowski, Frederick L., ed. *Administrative Uses for Microcomputers.* Three vols. Park Ridge, Ill: Research Corp. of the Association of School Business Officials of the U.S. and Canada, 1983.

Little, Joseph R., et al. *Micros for Managers.* Trenton, N.J.: New Jersey School Boards Association, 1984.

Mecklenberger, James A., ed. "Technology in Education." *Phi Delta Kappan*, September 1988.

Moursand, David. "New Views of Computer Literacy: The Computer as Tool." *The Practitioner*, December 1986. (Moursand is also the chief executive officer of the International Council for Computers in Education, publisher of another excellent journal, *The Computing Teacher*, available through the University of Oregon, 1787 Agate St., Eugene, Oreg. 97403.)

Pogrow, Stanley. *Evaluations of Educational Administration Software.* Tucson, Ariz.: Ed-Ad Systems, 1985.

CHAPTER 10
Personalized Education

JAMES W. KEEFE

AMERICAN SCHOOLS ARE generally successful. They are caring and well-meaning places, and they are usually safe and systematic. However, they are not always helpful and supportive for all students.

There is nothing wrong with the way American schools operate that a little long overdue modernizing would not fix. Everything in American schooling that is dysfunctional today was perfectly comprehensible and justifiable 100 years ago.

The problems of our schools reflect our goal to educate everyone to his or her potential. American schools are victims of their own best intentions. To realize their own highest aspirations, they need some systematic updating.

The conventional approach to reform in our schools has been to add more requirements or more programs. We are weighed down by an incremental approach to change. Rather than make deep and integrative changes, we tend to add more programs. We are "programmed" to death.

Well-intentioned governors and state legislatures are calling for more demanding forms of education. Their methods in many instances, however, are no more promising than existing practices. More of the same adds extra baggage rather than versatility and scope.

Reform efforts may be a useful stimulus to improvement, but the current kind of reform is clearly a two-edged sword. Increasing academic requirements can benefit the academically inclined while working to push others out of the system. In the most fundamental sense, a public system of education lacks utility unless the *majority* of young people can achieve some degree of success in it. Even instruction in the basic skills is meaningless for students who are unmotivated, unprepared, and ultimately unemployable. Outcome-based programs can be successful, but not without commitment to enhancing the learning skills of individual students. Personalizing schooling must be the highest priority for the 1980s and 1990s.

Schools are not organized for personalization. They are geared to crowds. Cusick (1973) calls this "batch processing." Many high schools, for example, are large, complex institutions. Administrators and teachers must deal with large numbers of students with limited time and resources. Expediency and efficiency are frequently better served in large schools than effectiveness. Miller (1980) put it aptly:

> . . . Batch processing influences classroom teaching. In order to process students for instruction, the school day is divided into discrete time periods, each devoted to individual subject matter instruction, with one teacher for every 25 students on the average . . . . This time structure makes teaching an activity that is performed in isolation from one's colleagues, invisible to one's peers. It also influences the type of instruction that occurs. Teaching approaches and methods which are most appropriate to the length of the period and the shape of the day are adopted; others are rejected as impractical.

Students who need a great deal of structure may be advantaged by "batching"; those who learn best in more flexible environments are significantly disadvantaged. *No matter what the economic or structural limitations of a school, a single approach to instruction, whether traditional or contemporary, simply does not do the job.*

Recent research in instructional diagnosis, methodology, and style is building a solid conceptual base for change in this conventional educational practice. To change vocabulary is much easier than to change practice. Contemporary terms like mastery learning, effective instruction, and time-on-task can be used to cloak conventional practice as easily as team teaching and small-group instruction were employed a decade ago. Personalizing education, however, is not jargon. It is a basic instructional premise that supports some of the most important instructional concepts ever to emerge.

Most American schools lack a systematic model of schooling. When new content is mandated or a special need is perceived, a program is added—usually as a distinct activity unrelated to the ongoing curriculum. Teaching and learning take place as they always have—in isolation behind the classroom door. Little real collaboration takes place among administrators and teachers. The norm is individual activity in one's own autonomous arena—territoriality refined to an art. Yet, much of what research tells us argues for collaborative planning of instruction, flexible arrangements of time and resources, systematic diagnosis of student capabilities, appropriate remediation of student cognitive skills, and a personalized approach to teaching and learning.

Characteristics of Personalized Education

All learning is entirely personal. Readiness and incentive, rate of learning, preferred methodology and content, all vary widely from person to person. Every learner has unique abilities, experiential background, and learning styles. No two learners are necessarily ready to learn at the same time or to the same degree. Learning for each individual is, to an extent, unique.

A personalized view of education requires that we accept students where they are (intellectually, socially, emotionally, physically) and help them to progress at their own rates and at an optimal level for their capabilities.

H. L. Mencken once said that "For every deep and complex problem facing our society there is a simple answer, and it's wrong."

Personalized education is that kind of complex problem, one whose solutions reflect an historical quest stretching back to the beginnings of the modern era. Many of the solutions for personalizing education have been simplistic, even monolithic, in their conceptualization. As a result, we are still looking.

Kasten (1986) and others report that school classrooms in America are remarkably similar:

> About 75 percent of class time is spent on instruction. The rest is spent in routines such as preparation for instruction, roll taking, and cleanup. About 70 percent of the class time involves oral interaction between students and teachers during which teachers outtalk students by about three to one. Teachers ask about five times as many direct questions as open questions. And most teacher talk is emotionally neutral . . . . Goodlad (1983) and his fellow researchers in *A Place Called School* concluded that life in most American classrooms is fundamentally boring.

Instructional planning must be based on an analysis of student characteristics. To do so would move education away from the traditional assembly line, batch processing model to a personalized one. Programs could then be based on the appropriate differences that exist among groups of learners rather than on the assumption that everybody learns the same way.

Personalized education is a systematic effort on the part of a school to take into account individual student characteristics and effective instructional practices in organizing the learning environment.

Carroll (1975) called it "an attempt to achieve a balance between the characteristics of the learner and the learning environment."

It is a match of the learning environment with the learner's knowledge, processing strategies, concepts, learning sets, motivational systems, and acquired skills. And it is a continual process.

Personalization differs in several important ways from traditional approaches to schooling. Let us take a few minutes to examine some of these differences. "Learning is a process (p) which occurs over some period of time (t) and always involves the individual learner (L) achieving some objective (O)" (Burns, 1974).

In traditional classroom instruction, all learners are treated as constants (c). Time and process are treated as constants. Only achievement is allowed to vary (v). Students who need more time or different treatment learn less and receive lower grades. (See Figure 1.)

Figure 1
Traditional Model

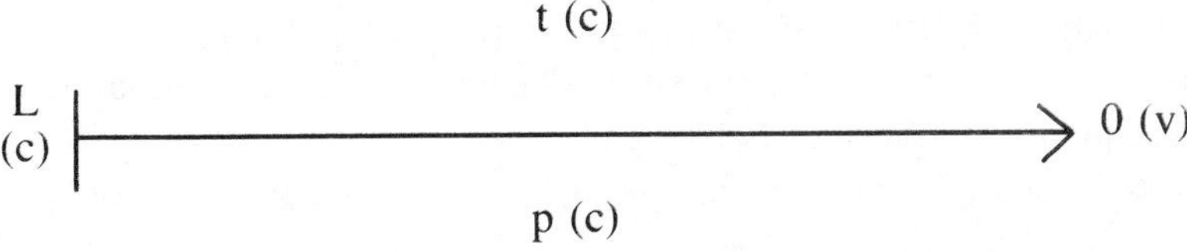

In personalized education, the learner is viewed as unique and, hence, variable (v). Time and process are allowed to vary within reasonable limits to encourage the individual learner to interact with available human and material resources—to achieve what is required at an acceptable level of performance or mastery. The interaction (I) of the learner with the process constitutes the essential foundation of personalization.

It is the role of the teacher to facilitate this interaction. The quality of personalization depends on the quality of this interaction, which in turn is dependent on the quality of available resources, both human and material. (See Figure 2.)

Figure 2
Personalized Model

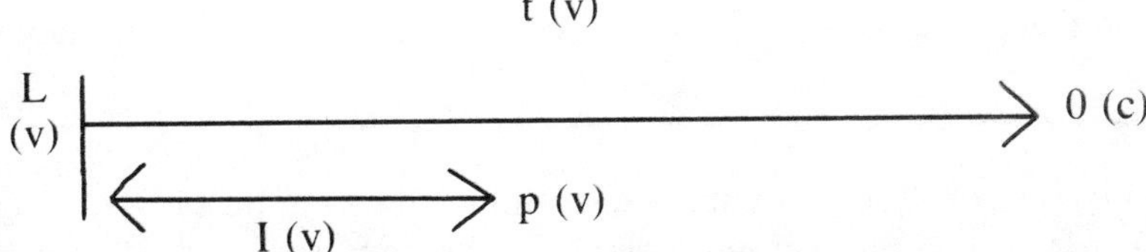

Contemporary research on learner and teacher characteristics supports a personalized approach—more precisely, a teaching-learning cycle of diagnosis, prescription, instruction, and evaluation (DPIE). The DPIE cycle has been explicit or implicit in every national educational reform project—from the Eight Year Study of 1933-1941, to the NASSP Model Schools Project (1969-1974), to contemporary research on time-on-task and direct instruction.

This writer formulated the following model of personalized education initially in the mid-1970s to flesh out the DPIE cycle for a follow-up group of schools from the Model Schools Project (the Learning Environments Consortium in the western states/provinces of the United States and Canada). The model incorporates the best of research-based strategies and proven classroom instructional components while leaving the mode of implementation to the school or district. It is both structured and flexible. It suggests a total teaching-learning plan for all students but requires no one approach for all.

The personalized education model has been revised several times in the past decade to reflect new and significant developments in educational diagnosis and delivery. (It will surely be revised again to remain current and useful.) The model calls for development of working components in 12 broad, related areas of the school program, each tied to one of the elements of the DPIE cycle.

Model of Personalized Education

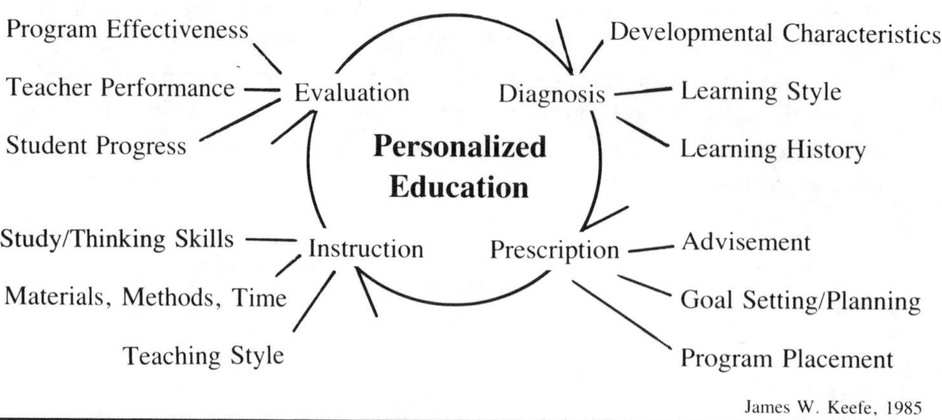

James W. Keefe, 1985

Diagnosis is concerned with student traits, learning problems, and the nature of the learning environment. It encompasses student developmental characteristics, learning history (Benjamin Bloom's term for acquired knowledge, skills, and attitudes), and learning style.

1. Developmental characteristics are those specific stages in individual maturation when certain capacities for learned behavior appear (e.g., visual perception, language pronunciation, reading, cognitive thinking skills). These characteristics tell us *when* a student is developmentally ready to learn something; they indicate individual physiological readiness for learning. Readiness signals the boundaries of learning potential.

2. Learning styles are characteristic cognitive, affective, and physiological behaviors that serve as relatively stable indicators of how students perceive, interact with, and respond to the learning environment. They can be measured by a variety of assessment techniques. Learning style tells us *how* a student learns and likes to learn. NASSP's *Learning Style Profile* (Keefe and Monk, 1986), for example, provides information on 24 independent style elements to assist teachers in planning instruction. Style analysis establishes the road map for learning and instruction.

3. Learning history reveals *what* a student knows and what his or her morale is at a given point in his or her learning career—the knowledge, skills, and school attitudes a learner possesses before entering on a new learning experience (Bloom, 1976). These attitudes and achievements may be measured by curriculum-referenced or normative (standardized) tests, attitudinal inventories, and biographical profiles of home and peer group influences (Walberg, 1988). Learning history determines the starting point for all subsequent learning and instruction.

Prescription is concerned with advisement, goal setting, program planning, and placement. Teachers help students set appropriate instructional objectives and activities, assist with grouping and scheduling arrangements, and provide ongoing advisement for small groups of students.

4. Advisement brings the student into continuous contact with persons, places, and activities that facilitate development of his or her talents and interests. The teacher adviser is the key person in this process (Keefe, 1984). Each student has an adult adviser in the school who is personally interested in his or her development.

5. Goal setting begins with a personal profile developed for each student from the diagnostic data available to professional counselors and teacher advisers. Students (and parents) meet with advisers for ongoing advisement. Program planning builds on the student's diagnostic profile and personal/career goals. Both one-year and three/four-year plans are developed. The three or four-year plan outlines long-range educational goals based on mutual agreement among parents, teachers, and the student. The one-year plan focuses on the student's program of study for the current year and any interventions that will enhance cognitive skills, study habits, and the use of out-of-school time.

6. Program placement involves scheduling the student in courses and learning activities with materials and methods appropriate for the individual's development, skill needs, and learning style. The school curriculum and schedule must provide both the structure and the flexibility for this purpose. (Block schedules are particularly suitable.) Resource teachers help with cognitive and academic diagnosis, skills training, and coaching.

Personalized instruction embraces teacher styles, teaching methodologies, time use, study and thinking skills. Teachers structure the learning environment, train students in study and thinking skills and time use, organize information, etc.

7. Teaching styles are characteristic instructional behaviors reflective of teacher personality and educational philosophy. Different teaching styles create different learning environments. Systematic views of teaching style have been proposed by Joyce and Weil (1979), and others. The most successful teachers use different styles in flexible ways. Research

indicates that effective instructional environments are characterized by teacher commitment to the norms of continual improvement and mutual collaboration (Little, 1981).

8. Different materials and methods are appropriate for different student styles, skills, and interests. A personalized approach can and should include tutorial or clinical coaching, computer-based instruction, individualized instruction, cooperative small group/team learning activities, experiential learning, mastery learning, direct instruction, adaptive instruction, lecture-recitation, etc. Instruction is monitored and students are given feedback on the effectiveness of their time use, and the quality of their academic achievement. Choice of materials and methods are determined by diagnosed student needs.

9. Study skills are basic mental tools that students use to obtain information (e.g., note taking). Thinking skills are developed mental *capabilities* that enable students to manipulate knowledge and experience. Functional study skills are prerequisite to a maturing learning style which in turn supports the growth of higher order thinking skills. Formal study and thinking skills training is important for all students, with practice and reinforcement in all the content areas. Cognitive resource teachers assist teachers in incorporating skills' diagnosis and training in subject matter instruction (Letteri, 1985).

Evaluation looks at the status of learners, teachers, and programs.

10. Student achievement is assessed and reported in terms of absolute performance, or skill standards, rather than relative criteria. Grades do not indicate class standing, but rather what a student has or has not learned.

11. Teacher evaluation assesses instructional competence and performance on mutually-agreed-upon goals. Some form of teacher self-appraisal and developmental supervision is an integral part of the improvement process. Administrator growth profiles help principals and vice principals identify personal strengths and weaknesses and work toward constructive goals.

12. The total school curriculum is evaluated in terms of district/school philosophy, goals, and objectives.

Feedback using data from student assessment, teacher appraisal, and program evaluation is the basis for: (a) continuation, modification, or termination of a given program; (b) continuing diagnosis of student needs; and (c) repetition of the entire DPIE cycle.

Some Ongoing Efforts

Several schools or systems have made progress in implementing elements of personalized education. Linganore High School in Frederick, Md., under the leadership of principal Kevin Castner, applied the model to improve the classroom grades of "on-grade" students. The implementation was designed in 1985 as a three to five-year project.

Although their participation in instructional change was voluntary, all teachers were exposed to the concepts of personalized education and Joyce and Showers' (1983) model of staff development. The Linganore personalized model called upon the professional staff to adjust classroom instruction to the needs of students. Teachers were asked to determine:

- The correct level of difficulty (rather than a different task) for each student
- The appropriate *learning* behaviors for each student in a deliberately arranged environment
- The appropriate *instructional* behaviors to facilitate achievement.

A staff survey conducted in 1986 showed that teachers accepted the concepts of personalized education as appropriate for the school, that techniques associated with the model were being more widely and successfully applied than before the project, and that student learning outcomes had improved. Student achievement was monitored in several ways through the fall of 1987, with the following results:

	1983		*1987*
School Average GPA	2.30		2.70
Honor Roll	244		497
Athletic Ineligibility (Two F's in a quarter)	190		77
Maryland Functional Tests			
Math	59%	Passing	80%
*Writing	48%	Passing	92%

* On-grade students improved in writing from 28% passing to 92%; remedial students, from 5% to 89%.

The Marion City (Ohio) Schools have used the personalized education model as a conceptual scheme to direct the rethinking of curricular and instructional practices in the district. Assistant Superintendent for Instruction John M. Conrath has focused efforts on student diagnosis, staff advisory functions, classroom level prescription, and instructional staff development.

A computerized learning style assessment program identifies student learning style and prints out a prescription sheet to assist teachers in classroom advisement, goal setting, and student placement. Each student is profiled by the Computerized Assessment of Student Attributes (CASA) that provides teachers with extensive information on student aptitude, achievement, learning style, and self-concept. Prescription either emphasizes enhancement of one of the student's learning style characteristics or learning/instruction based on diagnosed strengths.

Staff development has concentrated intensively on the instructional process, raising teacher awareness of learning style, teaching style, effective classroom management, cooperative learning, and learning center approaches. Future plans include attention to study and thinking skills training, and to the entire evaluation component of the personalized model.

Conclusion

The most significant unfinished agenda in American education is the need for the systemic personalization of schooling. Most American schools are loosely coupled organizations held together by highly individualistic teachers and administrators working largely in isolation from one another. Instruction is delivered primarily as lecture or discussion/recitation. Instructional focus is on the group and what a "typical student" can do. But no typical students really exist, only students who do well or less well in a particular learning environment.

American schools must be systematically reorganized to support instructional improvement, and American classrooms must become less rigid. For personalized education to work, at least eight elements of good curriculum and instructional planning must be institutionalized in schools and districts:

1. K-12 articulation of subject content from the bottom up
2. Systematic diagnosis of student development, style, attitudes, and skills
3. Ongoing advisement for all students
4. Collaborative teacher planning of instruction
5. Interactive learning environments providing for real dialog
6. Mastery-based instruction in basic skills
7. Cooperative small-group arrangements for conceptual learning and socialization
8. Objective assessment of student progress, and teacher and program performance.

Minimal structural changes might involve less rigid scheduling approaches (e.g., block schedules or schools within schools), regular advisement conferences for all students, more small-group interaction, and use of coaching techniques in instruction. The goal again would be to ensure that all students experience success, whatever their cognitive or affective skills and needs.

To work, a personalized approach must be given a chance. It must have the support of teachers, administrators, parents, and politicians. And it must be given time to take root and to grow in classrooms and schools. Personalized education is a truly modern response to the need for a systematic renewal of schooling. It should become our next serious goal for American education.

References

Bloom, B.S. *Human Characteristics and School Learning*. New York: McGraw-Hill, 1976.

Burns, R.W. "Interaction: Place Your Efforts Where the Action Is." *Educational Technology*, November 1974.

Carroll, A. W. *Personalizing Education in the Classroom*. Denver, Colo.: Love Publishing, 1975.

Cusick, P.A. *Inside High School*. New York: Holt, Rinehart and Winston, 1973.

Goodlad, J.I. *A Place Called School*. New York: McGraw-Hill, 1983.

Joyce, B., and Weil, M. *Models of Teaching*, 2nd ed. Englewood Cliffs, N.J.: Prentice-Hall, 1979.

Joyce, B., and Showers, P. *Power in Staff Development Through Research and Training*. Washington, D.C.: Association for Supervision and Curriculum Development, 1983.

Kasten, K. "Redesigning Teachers' Work." *Issues in Education,* Winter 1986.

Keefe, J.W. "Advisement." In *Instructional Leadership Handbook*, edited by J.W. Keefe and J.M. Jenkins. Reston, Va.: NASSP, 1984.

Keefe, J.W., and Monk, J.S. *Learning Style Profile* and *Examiner's Manual*. Reston, Va.: NASSP, 1986.

Letteri, C.A. "Teaching Students How To Learn." *Theory into Practice*, Spring 1985.

Little, J.W. *School Success and Staff Development: The Role of Staff Development in Urban Desegregated Schools*. Boulder, Colo.: Center for Action Research, 1981.

Miller, L. "The High School and Its Teachers: Implications for Staff Development." *Journal of Staff Development*, May 1980.

Walberg, Herbert J. "Creativity and Talent as Learning." In *The Nature of Creativity: Contemporary Psychological Perspectives*, edited by R.J. Sternberg. New York: Cambridge University Press, 1988.

CHAPTER 11

The Computerization of Schools

DUSTIN H. HEUSTON

THE COMMENTS IN this chapter are derived from the experiences of the Waterford School, a nonprofit experimental school in Provo, Utah, with more than 400 students in pre-school through grade 12. The Waterford School was founded in 1981 as a model school to use the most advanced computer technology wisely and well. The school was designed as a prototype for public schools.

Freedom to innovate has been maintained by having a nonprofit institute, the Waterford Institute, pay for the cost of the school. This funding has allowed the school to remain private and free of state regulations while attracting a parent body that is typical of the public schools.

The school opened in 1981 with kindergarten through grade 5, and in 1982 incorporated a middle school with grades 6 through 8. Beginning in 1983, the high school added a grade per year. The school graduated its first college-bound class in June 1987.

During the first fall semester, students were not allowed near computer terminals, and a careful effort was made to imitate the dynamics of a typical public school setting. The elementary school classes had 25 students per section, and most of the teachers were hired from local public schools. The students were not chosen for academic talents, but primarily for economic and social diversity.

The Waterford trustees decided to build an empirical model in which faculty members would determine the placement and traditions of usage for the work stations. After a traditional school had been running for a number of months, the first teminals were introduced to students in January 1982. Teachers decided, after considerable debate, to put the terminals in formal computer laboratories—traditional classrooms with 30 terminals in study carrels.

They also opted for a paraprofessional in the computer learning center to provide support and assistance in implementing the curriculum. The key concern was to avoid working with or thinking about the computer as technology, and instead to use the benefits of the technology in a way that supported the curriculum. As they expressed it, teachers wanted their experience to be "computer blind," to focus their energies on curriculum.

A thorough debate and analysis suggested a number of compelling reasons for having separate laboratories:

1. The terminals could be utilized 100 percent of the time in a formal laboratory setting. In a classroom setting, there would be many times when the terminals could not be used because the teacher would be working with the class as a whole or the students would not be in the classroom (lunch, physical education, etc.).
2. Teachers felt that they would have to become technologists if they were responsible for terminals in their classrooms. They worried about adequate training, support, and the stress of trying to use the terminals enough during the day to justify their presence in the classroom.
3. Teachers realized that if a few students were using the terminals in a classroom setting, they would still have to work with other subgroups. This would prevent them from observing interactions at the terminals that would help them understand student thought processes with the materials.

As one high school teacher commented after using the materials for a few years, "Eighty percent of the classroom time I used to spend introducing new material and doing theory. Now, it's a different role than I've ever been able to play before. In the computer lab, I walk around and watch the students and monitor their progress. It's *monitoring*; it's *coaching* more than instructing. I learn from the kids and see how they do things. Sometimes, they're amazingly insightful, and sometimes they think in ways you'd never think of. I am reaching more kids appropriately than I've ever reached before."

During the first year, teachers experienced a great deal of anxiety about using classroom time for the learning laboratory. They felt that it was dangerous to give up the precious time traditionally scheduled to teach the curriculum. They adopted a defensive strategy, sending only half a class to the laboratory while retaining half to work with them in the classroom. Losing classroom time would be compensated for by working with smaller groups on a more individual basis. Each student was sent to the learning center for half of a period (20 minutes), 10 minutes of which was spent working on math, and 10 minutes on language arts and reading.

Within a few months, it was obvious that students were learning so much from the computer that the routine was changed for the second year. Teachers brought entire classes to the learning center and combined their efforts with the paraprofessional for 40-minute sessions.

It should be noted that printed management reports showing how students were progressing in relation to curricular objectives had an extraordinary motivational effect on teachers. In a typical classroom setting, a teacher lecturing to a class as a whole cannot know in "real time" how each student is doing. The computer management reports showed precisely what was happening to each student in each session, and inevitably led teachers to call on the computer to give individual assistance to students.

Teachers were also pleased with the help given by laboratory managers. Together they motivated and helped one other as they attempted to individualize instruction. Within a few years, teachers requested that student time on the work stations be increased to about an hour a day. This pattern permitted the school to retain its normal academic schedule and traditions.

The elementary level population at Waterford has been relatively stable, so research on these grades has been quite reliable. At the end of six years, a total gain of approximately 40 percent was evident on the Iowa Test of Basic Skills. The specific breakdown is as follows:

	1981 (opening)	*1987*	*% Gain*
Math	59 percentile	95 percentile	61%
Language Arts	69 percentile	92 percentile	33%
Reading	73 percentile	91 percentile	25%

The results in the high school have been no less impressive, but with some attrition, the population represented is slightly less than 100 students:

- The senior class of 23 students has four National Merit finalists.
- In 1988, Waterford took first place among schools in the state in math. The highest score in the high school division and the two highest scores in the junior high division were from Waterford.
- In 1988, 42 students in Utah scored in the 90th percentile of the 32,000 students taking the German exam nationally. Ten were from Waterford. In subsequent tests, Waterford students placed first and third in the Senior Division, and first, third, and fourth in the Junior Division. Waterford was named the top school in the state.
- In 1988, in the state French contest, 11 of 12 Waterford students achieved the highest (superior) rating and 4 won first place in divisional contests.

College acceptances have been very impressive for a small Utah town with a population of approximately 70,000. Students have been accepted at Brandeis, Brigham Young, Brown, Cornell, Dartmouth, Harvey Mudd, Johns Hopkins, Mills, Oberlin, Pennsylvania, Rice, St. Johns College, Southern California, Utah, Wellesley, and Yale, among others. Almost all Waterford students have gone on to college.

The Contributions of the Computer Curriculum

The value of the computer follows from its ability to support teachers in instructional tasks. Some of the contributions of the computer are:

- The ability to increase individual instruction. Most teachers and administrators are unaware that the average public school student in the United States receives only one minute a day of individual instruction. This adds up to half a day a year, and slightly less than a week for all of elementary and secondary schooling. Two studies have corroborated this, the latest by Eaton Conant (1973).

At the Waterford School, student activity on the work stations is very individualized. The programs provide trials with feedback, tutorial help, and appropriate branching, depending on student responses. Assuming that 10 minutes of a typical hour is spent in daydreaming or socialization, the computer is still providing 50 minutes of individual instruction, or 50 times the national average. This extraordinary increase in individualization has very positive educational effects.

- The instructional materials have been carefully sequenced by objective so that students are assured of mastery if they work through the sequence in a responsible manner. Students who have missed classes or are moving at a different pace than the class as a whole are guaranteed the opportunity to learn the materials.
- Work stations allow students to work in private without public scrutiny. This privacy protects slow learners who may be embarrassed by trying and failing, as well as bright students who are frequently harassed by their peers if they perform at too high a level.
- The computer curricula have been designed to offer materials in more than one mode. In the high school algebra course, for example, materials are presented in standard equations, but also in X-Y coordinate graphic format. This allows both right and left brain dominant students to learn the materials more easily.

One high school teacher from Waterford commented:

> When there is just a teacher and a textbook, teachers usually try to 'teach to the book'—to teach things the way the book does it. But when there is (1) the book, (2) the computer, and (3) the teacher, the computer often does it a little differently from the book, and I can do it differently than both of them. So, the kids get three ways to understand, and the one they actually get is still a fourth—their own! It's a team teaching process, with the student and the computer as members of the team.

Another teacher added:

> When students see things for the first time on the computer, or in class for that matter, they often need to see it again. And it helps for them to see it in a different way, in a different presentation. The courseware provides an alternative window on the same thing I teach in class. It doesn't take anything away from my presentation if the computer does it first; more kids just understand, and they don't get bored because my way is a little different. Most kids need to see things more than once and from several different approaches.

- The computer curriculum leads to a much deeper understanding of the materials and allows teachers to emphasize higher order thinking skills instead of just teaching the rudimentary basics. A high school math teacher commented:

> You can't do much with higher-order understandings if students don't know the basics; but the basics also aren't much good if you never get to the higher-order stuff—like applications and problem solving. That's the problem! In the past, I had to pick one or the other. But with the computer, for the first time I can do both. In fact, my students now cover everything that we used to do in about two-thirds the time. So I can say to myself, "Now what do you want to do?" I'm doing lots of things I've never been able to do before.

Research Results in Public School Districts

The Waterford School laboratory model has been used by many school districts across the United States. Currently there are more than 400 sites with the WICAT professional systems that Waterford chose (as vendor) for its laboratory course materials. Most of the research data on the program come from elementary and middle schools because computer courseware evolved from elementary to secondary.

Recently, however, excellent high school materials have been developed in geometry, algebra, trigonometry, pre-calculus, writing, grammar, language arts, chemistry, Pascal, BASIC, at-risk programs, adult remediation, typing, and GED preparation. These courses are rich and varied in their content, and require professional (mainframe) systems to run.

The chemistry course, for example, is 80 megabytes (80 million characters), and the "help features" alone would require more than 200 diskettes if they were stored for a personal computer. As time goes on, high schools will see the same type of learning gains achieved by elementary and middle schools with their earlier deployment of learning laboratories.

Waterford School Recommendations

In talking with scores of professional educators from various school districts who have visited, Waterford personnel have noted some common misunderstandings that appear to diminish the full potential of computer use available to schools.

1. Confusion about technologies is widespread. Many administrators view computers as "another" technology. They miss the distinguishing characteristic of the computer that makes it fundamentally different from any other technology. Properly programmed, a computer is a source of artificial intelligence capable of interacting with students in a private instructional mode.

The student is pushed into an active role through a series of trials, with feedback initiated by the computer. Every other technology keeps the learner passive. The great contribution of the computer is that it forces a learner to be active. Productivity is much greater than with standard technologies such as television, videotapes, cassettes, slide tapes, etc., which basically replicate the teacher.

2. Computer functions have not been clearly understood or their priorities assessed by districts. Some of these uses are:

- Teaching computer literacy
- Teaching computer programming
- Solving district data processing needs
- Teaching spread sheets and other business functions
- Teaching typing
- Improving the effectiveness of instruction.

Different types of computer technologies are appropriate, depending on the function. A personal computer (PC) is excellent for teaching computer literacy, and can be used in laboratories for teaching word processing or spread sheets. But a PC is not a good device for district data processing unless it is connected to a file server with appropriate management and testing software. Vendors interested in selling PCs would have districts believe otherwise.

To have a strong instructional impact on students, programs must be very large, rich, and carefully crafted to provide a variety of branching responses for student interactions. They must be able to track every keystroke, call in tutorial aids, produce reports, and generally support teachers and students in a broad range of instructional tasks. A number of vendors are now selling professional systems that can use their own terminals or PCs as work stations. Unless a district works with one of these vendors, it will not be able to obtain programs that will generate significant instructional gains.

Once a district has determined to use computers for serious instructional improvement, then it is important that instructional experts become involved in the decision-making process. If decisions are left exclusively to data processing centers or high school business education departments, some wrong choices will inevitably be made.

3. Some institutions are so enamored of technology that they miss the centrality of the computer work station. The videodisc will be an important instructional device at some point in the future. Recognizing this, the Waterford Institute developed a number of the first educational videodiscs. But emphasis on vidediscs, CDROMs, cable TV, satellites, or national networks can sidetrack district efforts from the core task.

Waterford staff members believe that schools should use standard terminal work stations connected to courseware systems and file servers that can teach many of the standard materials in English, writing, reading, and mathematics. Schools will find that they need many more work stations than they currently anticipate so every effort should be made to avoid expensive components like videodiscs. A good rule of thumb is that a 30-terminal system can serve about 400 students for 20-30 minutes of instruction a day. The cost of work stations, file server, maintenance, and leasing course materials is about $50 per year per student. Moreover, as students improve with the help of professional systems, schools need to increase the time spent on terminals to about an hour a day.

When districts understand the full potential of computers, they will begin to view them as a useful optional methodology for reaching instructional goals with far less investment. One district, for example, determined that its instructional improvement goals would cost taxpayers an additional $50 million for special programs, small class sizes, and remediation centers. It found that it could achieve the same instructional gains by spending $10 million, or 20 percent of the original budget, on work stations. The computer option has been very effective in reaching their instructional goals.

In the future, districts with class size flexibility, by adding one or two students per class and utilizing computers effectively, will be able to offer greater individualization. The financial savings generated by slightly larger sections will not only pay for the use of the computers, but generate additional revenue for salaries or other fiscal needs.

Reference

Conant, E. H. *Teacher and Paraprofessional Work Productivity*. Lexington, Mass.: Lexington Books (D.C. Heath), 1973.

CHAPTER 12

A School for 2088

FENWICK W. ENGLISH

LET US MOVE time like a chess piece, forward and back, to carry out a strategy of the mind. Imagine for a moment, moving our chess piece backward 100 years to 1888, and trying to explain to an adult who lived then what life is like in 1988.

Adults then might have understood automobiles, but streams of super-highways curling around most of the major megalopolises? What about television, rockets, and space travel? Now try radar and lasers, and even laser surgery. Think about the looks of disbelief at test tube babies and starwar defense systems, at transistors, and at computers in millions of private homes. Would they believe that most of the childhood diseases would be eradicated by something called antibiotics discovered from pumpkin mold? The nineteenth century adult would find most of our everyday experiences simply preposterous.

Now move the chess piece forward the same amount of time. We are now visiting an educational colony of the 21st century, in the year 2088. The educational colony has replaced the school—the idea of the past several centuries.

Our host is Robert Applegate, a sympathetic and patient equivalent of the 20th century principal. He understands our mission and has agreed to provide us with a brief tour.

"That's the school?" I asked.

"Well, not exactly," said Applegate. "It contains elements you may recognize from your time as part of a school, but I think you will see something different."

"It's huge and it has no form. There are no windows. It must be at least 12 stories high. What's in there?"

"Here," he motioned, "we'll go into the colony through this time zone." With that, Applegate took us through a curtained entrance and we stepped out to a hewn-rock street. I gazed around.

"This isn't the 21st century, it's more like the 1st or 2nd century."

"Not bad," said Applegate. "Actually it's 3 A.D., to be exact. Our students are immersed in the Roman period for a month."

"You mean they study in here?"

"No, more correctly, they live in here for a month. You knew back in the 20th century that total immersion quickened learning. You even tried it with some magnet schools. But there was nothing like this then.

Here it is possible to literally transport students back into a historical period exactly as it was at that time.''

''Where is this place?'' I asked.

''Jerusalem. We entered near the Plaza column. To the immediate right is the Cardo, the road that goes by the Temple of Aphrodite. Off to the far right you may be able to make out the camp of the Tenth Roman Legion. To the left on that high ground is the Temple of Jupiter.'' (Bahat, 1986).

''Why Jerusalem? Why not Rome?''

''Jerusalem is manageable given our square footage. Rome would be wonderful, but it is simply beyond our budget. Besides, the archaeological evidence about Jerusalem has been nearly unraveled. So we have been able to reconstruct the time quite well. Our students work and live out the controversies of that period.''

''This is incredible. It's like a movie set.''

''It's better,'' commented our futuristic principal. ''It was planned in our computer-assisted curriculum design shop by our own staff. A couple of our seniors assisted in the reconstruction of the market junction, which is directly ahead. These are the two main thoroughfares of Hadrian's Jerusalem which was then called 'Aelia Capitolina.' One of these seniors is going to major in educational culture design. He won a scholarship for the research that went into that piece.''

''How is instruction carried on?''

''In Latin,'' smiled Applegate. ''We've always known that language and culture were inseparable, but the interlock of language learning with culture for students not native to that language was not fully understood until well-developed theories of cognition were tested in laboratories at the beginning of the 21st century.''

''Was that known to us in 1988?''

''Yes,'' answered Applegate, ''even earlier. In 1983, a Professor Anderson at Carnegie Mellon wrote a book, *The Architecture of Cognition*. This book was a start in building a unified theory of cognition and then reconstructing it on a computer. That enabled us to build computers free of human programs.

''One of the first ones was named 'Soar'. What it did was enable a computer, free of a conventional program, to transfer previous learning from one situation to another while continuing to learn. In your time, it was called chunking (Wheeler, 1988).

''Now we call it 'patterning'. It is the equivalent of being in a maze and learning a language to get out of the maze at the same time. Because we understand the process and can recreate it, we have been able to speed up language acquisition in education. We can repeat the cycle of language acquisition of the early years of human life, ages one through five, many times prior to graduation. So most of our students speak four to five languages rather fluently. And they have learned them in context, as you did in learning one language in childhood.''

''After Latin, what languages do they learn? French? Spanish?''

''Not really, unless they want to major in classical languages. Most of our students learn Japanese, Chinese, Indonesian. This is the age of the Pacific Ring.

''The world has changed. It was changing in your time. For a long time, its centers were New York, London, and Paris. Now, of course, it's Los Angeles, Singapore, and Tokyo.''

''What about the curriculum here? Is it mostly social studies with some of the other subjects built in?''

Applegate stopped abruptly. I could tell I had rather irritated him with that question.

He looked at me quite seriously and said, ''Subjects as you knew them in the late 20th century, anachronisms even then, were abolished by national mandate in the great educational reforms at the beginning of the Thompson Presidency. About 2040-41, I guess.

''That was the time when education was centralized following the passage of the thirty-second amendment to the Constitution, making education a federal rather than a state responsibility.''

The shock on my face gave away my feelings. Applegate became more sympathetic.

''Really,'' he said, ''it's better. The subject-centered curriculum was the offshoot of 'faculty psychology', which was defunct in your times. You carried the form without the theory from which it had sprung. What finally brought it to a head was several decades of testing, showing conclusively that test scores were not improved until schools implemented radical new forms based on a solid knowledge about learning.''

''Like total immersion,'' I said.

''Yes.''

We walked down the Cardo, peering at students working on a variety of projects and activities.

''I'm going to take you to our curriculum/class set design center. It's beyond the Tetrapylon just ahead.''

We entered a room that had very large screens with grids imposed on them. Computer consoles were everywhere. In the next room were what appeared to be disk replication apparatus and printing facilities.

''Let me introduce you to our curriculum set designer, Dr. Grey.'' Dr. Grey was a woman who shook my hand and motioned me to a sound booth, so as not to interrupt the discussion going on in the center.

''Hello. Bob told me about you. What you see here is the control room for curriculum set design. On Friday we are going to strike the Roman/Jerusalem set. We are in the final stages of scenario construction for studying crisis at the community level. That will be up on Monday.''

''This whole thing will be gone then?'' I asked.

''Correct. We have some storage capabilities here. Some will be taken by truck to central district storage for use next year. Would you like to know how we go about scenario construction?''

I nodded.

''A scenario is a chunk of curriculum that is totally replicated in a living environment, just like the one you saw outside for Jerusalem. The scenario replaced the old static concept of a curriculum unit used in the 20th century.

''What the scenario does is to take several data streams from our computer bank and configure them around a concrete, live environment. The data streams relate to the basic characteristics of the learners and the learning environments they have experienced before, both in and out of school. They create a match between student knowledge, personal processing strategies, motivational proclivities, and learning orientations within a time-space relational context.

''This is the master curriculum core. From the core, several main and branching derivatives are developed. These are the scenarios. Each one is committed to disk and placed in the teachers' individual instructional computer systems. They are also printed prior to starting the experience.''

Searching for the proper vocabulary to avoid appearing outdated or awkward, I questioned. ''What's the new set about?''

''Ah, we are moving into a fascinating time period, the Salem witch trials of 1692'' (Davidson and Lytle, 1986).

''But that was a mere aberration of the times,'' I noted. ''Surely there are a lot more important events to study.''

''An aberration, yes, but an extremely important and well-researched one,'' smiled Dr. Grey. ''It's a powerful scenario about a community in crisis, and it involves students in a way few others can. It is particularly effective for students who come to us alienated by environmental factors not traditionally embraced by schools.''

''How is that?'' I questioned.

''Well, we now know that the witch trials were the result of economic conflict between two parts of old Salem. These two parts were at odds with one another for more than 20 years; sort of 'ins' and 'outs', if you will.

''Most of the witches were women, and a large majority were widows or females of substance. Their freedom from dependence in a male-dominated society was a decided threat to that society. The phenomenon of the witch trials was no accident. It was a conflict rooted in greed, distribution of wealth, and sexism'' (Davison and Lytle, 1986, pp. 53-55).

''Students who are alienated must really identify with the witches,'' I commented.

''Right. But they do more than identify. This scenario is a powerful way to re-examine one's feelings about personal locus of control and the nature of social aggression and conflict. It is also tied up with cultural determinants, value and social codes, peer-group conformity patterns, and in-group, out-group conflict. Some of the more predatory social-economic patterns of society can be superbly lived and learned in the Salem witch trial scenario."

"When did these practices come into schools?" I asked.

"In your times," she answered, "with the expansion and maturation of learning style theory (Keefe, 1987). Some really significant breakthroughs occurred after the turn of the century, however. That really propelled the theory into practice."

"What were those?"

"Well, first, although it was well-established that socioeconomic status was predictive of school achievement and that I.Q. testing could be a means of retaining a caste structure (Gould, 1981), educators did not understand how much schools actually reinforced social inequality through classroom practices. These linkages were first explored in your times (Giroux, 1983) with a variety of studies on the hidden curriculum.

"Hidden curriculum meant the assumptions, methods, practices, and curricular content that passed on a mind set for social inequity so that the existing social order appeared inevitable, even 'natural'.

"Knowledge of the hidden curriculum freed educators from being 'anti-poor' in their educational practices. You see, if school emphasizes analytical skills, but the large mass of students are nonanalytical in their orientation, the school has constructed a curriculum and educational context that is abrasively discriminatory against that majority. If educational practices favor one race, or sex, or socioeconomic level, then they cannot be effective in erasing the larger societal trends that maintain a specific social order. When our schools were 'de-coupled' from this social morass, they became truly democratic."

"And the breakthrough for this?" I questioned.

"It was partly technological—that is, cybernetic—and partly theoretical. The testing ideology of the 19th and 20th centuries had to die and it did. But what really pushed it into oblivion was the technology that permits us today to construct curricular scenarios—a dynamic and fluid concept—instead of units which were essentially static.

"We can mix our curricular scenarios anyway you like, based on the number and types of learners, their prior learning environments, and the orientation of the curriculum to desired outcomes."

"You mean you can structure curriculum based on raw data?"

"Yes. It would be the equivalent of class scheduling in your times, developing a master schedule from a specified amount of input. However, your scheduling technologies were primitive compared to those we use routinely today."

"Who . . . where . . . does this happen?"

"That's right next door. Let me take you to our educational synthesis section.'' With that, Grey and Applegate escorted me to what must be the inner sanctum of the school of the 21st century, the synthesis section. There, master specialist Ann McTeer showed us the data storage room.

''In this room are the files of more than 50,000 students who have lived and learned here. Each file is contained on a chip about the size of a penny. Here, let's pick one at random and I'll show you.''

With that she punched into a device a series of numbers and the screen at the far end of the room lit up.

File 289-210-31128, Collins, Roger. Then the screen filled with data.

''What's all that?'' I asked.

Dr. Grey replied, ''Those data on the left of the boy's picture indicate his preferred information processing habits during the first review period. Let's see, at entry Roger was decidedly visual/spatial in his dominant sensory information processing response, followed by kinesthetic. Weakest was his auditory/verbal. He tended to stay with his dominant preference until almost overwhelmed by failure to respond. He had a low tolerance for new experiences. See, his capability index shows a strong perceptual-motor cue preference. That partially explains his lack of flexibility at that point.''

''All of that information is there?''

''Yes, it's coded, but it's there,'' answered Dr. Grey. ''Want to see Roger in action then?''

''Well, yes,'' I said.

''Let's see, first action taken of Roger is sub-file l5.'' She punched in the information and the screen showed Roger Collins working in what looked like an art class.

''Notice,'' intoned Ann McTeer, ''he's definitely visual/spatial and kinesthetic. Watch him with this task. Now watch as the task is changed. See how he keeps using the old dominant mode.''

''He's starting to get frustrated. Whoa, he's crying.''

''Right,'' noted Dr. Grey. ''I don't know if this clip will show when he changes his orientation.''

''How many clips like that are in this file?'' I asked.

''The typical student has maybe two dozen during the schooling period,'' said Applegate. ''The visual data base allows us to capture holistically both the student and the learning context at the points of greatest success or failure.''

''Do you use these in parent conferences?'' I asked.

''All the time. We also train parents to observe their children and discover how they can help in structuring experiences at home to strengthen weak areas that we are working on at school.''

''That's fantastic, incredible,'' I said. ''I can't wait to see what the classroom of the 21st century looks like. Let's go see one.''

There was a silence. ''Well, why don't you tell him, Bob,'' said McTeer with a half-smile.

''Ok, ok,'' responded Applegate, ''There aren't any, at least not the way you think of classrooms.''

''What, no classrooms? How can there be a school without classrooms? No classrooms, no teaching. Who teaches here, anyway? Where does it happen?''

''Your classroom of the 20th century was immobile. It was based on ideas of building utilization that originated in the Gary, Ind. platoon school concept (Spain, 1925). That approach compared to what we do today would be like equating the operation of a blacksmith shop with this synthesis center.''

''It's another anachronism,'' said Applegate. He was on the verge of lecturing me and was having a hard time finding the right metaphor to create the necessary time bridge for me.

''Ah,'' he said, ''in your times, do you remember...Disney World, the Epcot Center in Florida, things like that?''

''Yes.''

''Were there any classrooms at Epcot?''

''There weren't any, as I recall. The whole thing was just fluid movement.''

''Well,'' sighed Applegate, ''That's about as close to a school without classrooms in the 21st century as you could get in the 20th century.''

''But Disney World wasn't a school,'' I protested, emphasizing the word school.

''True enough,'' said Applegate, ''but did you learn a lot of things there?''

''Of course, but it was mostly entertainment; I mean, whatever was learned there was in the context of being entertained.''

''The same feeling you had when you walked on the Cardo this morning?'' asked Grey.

''Well, yes, I guess, the same feel. It was fun, an adventure, but that's not a school,'' I said again.

''It wasn't a school in your times because the metaphor for schooling was derived from 19th century factories rooted in standardization, stop and go assembly line routines, machine models for learning, and very high failure and dropout rates,'' said Grey.

''Yes, yes,'' I said, pausing. ''We didn't know any better.''

''That's not true,'' shot in Applegate. ''With the exception of the pure technology, everything we're doing now was in existence then, at least the ideas and concepts, as far back as the 1980s.''

''Maybe so,'' I shrugged, ''but nobody would have done this then. There was only one Epcot Center, and it was thought of as part of a big amusement park, not a school.''

''School really isn't like an amusement park now,'' cautioned McTeer, ''but it's the closest your 20th century experience would come to what we have today.''

''Do teachers still teach kids things?'' I questioned.

''Of course, but not in little boxes with 20 or 30 seats in neat little rows,'' smiled McTeer.

''Well, we were getting away from that in our more modern schools,'' I said, sounding a bit sarcastic, but adding, ''although not very much beyond that. What I don't understand is how you moved to this from where we were then?''

''You could have done it then,'' enjoined Applegate. ''No great wizardry was required. You could have done it.''

''That's like saying Leonardo could have flown in a 747 just because he designed a flying machine,'' I said, hoping to elicit a little understanding.

''Leonardo was a mind of his times, but he imagined beyond his times,'' commented Applegate. ''Once the technology was there, Leonardo's dream was a reality.''

''History shows us now that the 1980s were not times of imagination. They were for the most part times of consolidation, despite the fact that most of the ideas here were really known then. Now the 1990s, that was another decade!'' said Dr. Grey, shaking her head.

''I guess that was true enough,'' I agreed. ''We weren't very imaginative. We were too concerned with standards, test scores, and essentially unidimensional measures of learning.''

But perhaps wanting to know who were the missed prophets of the age, I asked, ''Was anybody worth listening to then?''

''Yes, of course,'' smiled Applegate. ''The giants of our time were influenced by several persons, but we can't tell you. The answers are embedded in time that has not yet passed. Imagination illuminates sometimes and lets one see far ahead, but it doesn't always explain.

''Understanding comes much more slowly and is laced with false starts and failure. The real trick is to know which prophets of one's times will last into the next. Historically, humans have had difficulty discerning popularity from wisdom'' (Tuchman, 1984).

So I ended my journey by moving the chess piece back. I began another search by examining the board and the possibilities which are here now, but could be extended into the future.

If your mind can imagine something, it can happen in the future. The future is always inherent in the lived consciousness of the moment. The school of 2088 is here now in its potential. It is up to us to find it.

References

Anderson, J.R. *The Architecture of Cognition*. Cambridge, Mass.: Harvard University Press, 1983.

Bahat, D. *Jerusalem*. Jerusalem, Israel: Carta, 1986.

Davidson, J.W., and Lytle, M.H. *After the Fact*. New York: Alfred A. Knopf, 1986.

Giroux, H.A. *Theory and Resistance in Education*. South Hadley, Mass.: Bergin and Garvey, 1983.

Gould, S.J. *The Mismeasure of Man*. New York: W.W. Norton and Co., 1981.

Keefe, J.W. *Learning Styles: Theory and Practice*. Reston, Va.: National Association of Secondary School Principals, 1987.

Spain, C.L. *The Platoon School: A Study of the Adaptation of the Elementary School Organization to the Curriculum*. New York: The Macmillan Co., 1925.

Tuchman, B.W. *The March of Folly*. New York: Ballantine Books, 1984.

Wheeler, D.L. "From Years of Work in Psychology and Computer Science, Scientists Build Theories of Thinking and Learning." *The Chronicle of Higher Education*, March 9, 1988.

CHAPTER 13

Multiple Perspectives on Organizing for Learning

JOHN J. LANE AND HERBERT J. WALBERG

"TRANSMIT CULTURE AND develop individuals."

"Make the school effective and efficient."

"Run a tight ship and develop a learning community."

The public wants it all. How can principals respond to so many conflicting demands? In particular, how should principals organize schools for learning?

The contributors to this book describe a dozen ways to organize schools. Some build on traditional models of school organization; others are futuristic. At the outset, Theodore Sizer reminds us that, even among good schools, no two are ever quite alike.

Still, we find more than a dozen themes or features among the diverse perspectives represented in the chapters. Several ideas and strategies appear in 5 to 12 chapters, no matter how distinctive the proposal for organizing learning. The themes are as follows:

- *Choice*—an alternative to geographical assignment; a voluntary means of matching students with school offerings.
- *Teacher Assignment*—the principal's authority to assign staff with as few restrictions as possible.
- *Principal Leadership*—the principal's ability to articulate and implement a vision of the school; also, principal visibility.
- *Change Culture*—an ethos of creation, innovation, and risk taking.
- *Personalized Learning*—research-based efforts to help students progress at rates appropriate to their maturational, intellectual, social, emotional, and physical abilities.
- *Staff Involvement*—the extent to which teachers and other staff are involved in key school decisions.
- *Parental Involvement*—the extent to which parents are involved in school decisions; also, parent participation in volunteer programs and "the curriculum of the home."
- *Technology*—the use of audiovisual materials, computers, and other electronic aids.
- *Curriculum Alignment*—the articulation of curriculum and classroom instruction with the evaluation system.
- *Effective School*—schools organized on the basis of a growing body of research about what makes schools effective.

- *Excellence*—concern with issues of quality in schools; e.g., increasing educational standards and challenging students to excel.
- *Diversity*—a "schooling for all" philosophy, embedded in democratic and republican understandings of citizenship.
- *Skill Mastery*—an emphasis on fundamentals, especially in reading and mathematics.

The chart shows which chapters emphasize these themes. It serves as a selective summary of the chapters and indicates the frequency of the recurrent features. Readers may use it as a chapter index to the features that appeal to them, or better, as a framework for developing and evaluating their own visions of organizing for learning.

Models and Features of Organization

Feature / Model	Choice	Teacher Assignment	Principal Leadership	Change-Culture	Personalized Learning	Staff Involvement	Parental/ Community Involvement	Technology	Curriculum Alignment	Effectiveness	Excellence	Diversity	Skill Mastery
Essential		X	X	X	X	X	X	X		X	X	X	X
James Madison			X			X	X		X		X	X	X
Site-Managed	X	X	X	X		X	X					X	
Mandate-Responsive	X			X		X	X		X	X	X	X	
Theory-Based		X	X	X		X			X				
Effective	X	X	X	X	X	X	X			X		X	X
Schools-Within-School		X		X	X	X	X	X	X		X		
Restructured	X	X	X	X	X	X	X			X	X	X	X
Information-Age			X			X		X	X				
Personalized			X	X	X	X		X	X	X	X	X	X
Computerized					X	X		X	X				X
2008			X	X	X	X	X	X	X			X	X
Totals	4	6	9	9	7	12	8	6	8	5	6	8	7